Joan Of Arc: Or, The Maid Of Orleans: From Michelet's History Of France...

Jules Michelet

Edith Rotch,
Nov.ᵣ 1859.

Joan of Arc:

OR,

The Maid of Orleans.

FROM

Michelet's History of France.

New York:
STANFORD & DELISSER, 508 Broadway.
1858.

PREFACE.

Our prosy American homes need to be illuminated by the presence of heroines and of heroes. Long enough have the shadows of the bloodless personages of mere fiction rested upon the hearthstone. Life and history are always stranger than the day-dreams of fancy; they can satisfy the cravings of imagination, while they feed the heart and instruct the mind. We hunger for the real, and our souls grow strong when nourished with "deeds sublime."

In our little "Household Library," we offer to all, portraits of the world's most heroic spirits, drawn by the most skilful hands. We begin with a woman, — Joan of Arc, the Maid of Orleans. Her Life is the most

(iii)

brilliant chapter in Michelet's brilliant History of France. You have it here, reader, in large, clear type, and can easily peruse it, while sitting at home or riding along the dusty highway. If the true story of that child of France does not make your heart strangely beat, then go your way, — hoe your corn or wash your dishes, count your cash or return Mrs. Grundy's call, cut a coat or sew a shirt, write a brief or give the finishing touch of educational death to a beautiful young soul, — there is no latent heroism, no latent romance, in you; it is impossible to awaken in you — not what sleeps, but what exists not, for it is not given to mortal to create something out of nothing.

Accept, then, all you that are worthy, — and we take comfort in believing that you are the majority, — this picture of feminine heroism. The life of Joan of Arc reveals to us the heart of France, and prophecies to us, more clearly than the philosophic words of any statesman, the future of that great people. America, too, in due time, shall have her Maid of Orleans, to represent the noblest, purest womanhood that history has yet developed. The cry of protest, raised here and there with more or less wisdom, or folly, points to a future that is not without hope.

Everybody in this country has heard of M. Michelet, but very few know any thing about him. A brief sketch of his life, we think, will be interesting to many.

Jules Michelet was born at Paris, August 21, 1798. In 1821, he entered upon a career of instruction, under the happiest auspices. From that period to the year 1826, he was successively employed at the Collége Rollin as teacher of history, of ancient languages, and of philosophy. In 1827 he was appointed *Maitre des Conferences* at the École Normale. Shortly after the revolution of July he was placed at the head of the historical department of the National Archives. In 1838 he succeeded Daunau in the chair of history and moral philosophy in the Collége de France. He was elected the same year a Member of the Institute, in the class of Moral Sciences.

The following are M. Michelet's principal works:—"Chronological *Tableau* of Modern History" (1825), "Synchronical *Tableau* of Modern History" (1826), and a "Summary of Modern History," "Introduction to Universal History" (1831), "Roman History" (same year), "Summary of the History of France before the Revolution" (1833), "*Œuvres Choisies*" from Vico, and "*Mémoires* of Luther," written by himself (1835), "Origin of French law *(droit)* sought in the symbols and formulas of universal law" (1837), "Jesuites" (1843), "The Priest, Woman, and the Family" (1844), "The People" (1846), the first volume of his "History of the Revolution" (1847). M. Michelet's great work is his "History of France," a new volume of which is just published. A recent production, entitled "*L'Oiseau,*" is full of poetry and melancholy, and perhaps reveals the heart of a man who has toiled and suffered much.

Gladly would we trace the celebrated historian through the struggles of his youth and the labors of his manhood; gladly would we endeavor to portray him as he has lived and worked in the midst of his cotemporaries, but limits are imposed upon us here, and we must content ourselves with the merest outlines. He was too liberal for even the government of Louis Philippe, which deprived him of his professor's chair. After the revolution of February, he returned to his chair, but the government silenced him again, in 1850. He lost his place in the Archives when, after the *Coup d'Etat* of December, 1851, he refused to take the oath of allegiance to the perjured usurper of the throne of France. His country, on whose fair bosom rests for a period a frightful military incubus, must be deprived of the services of her noblest sons. Vain, however, are the despot's proscriptions. Others, as well as M. Guizot, can repeat the significant language of M. de Châteaubriand: "When, in the silence of abject submission, we hear only the chains of the slave and the voice of the informer; when all tremble before the tyrant, and it is as dangerous to incur favor as to merit disgrace, the historian appears to be charged with the vengeance of nations. It is in vain that Nero triumphs. Tacitus has been born in the Empire; he grows up near the ashes of Germanicus, and already uncompromising Providence has handed over to an obscure child the glory of the master of the world."

This Life of Joan of Arc is a fair specimen of M. Michelet's fervid, poetical style. Most of the foot-notes, which are without interest for any but historical scholars, have been omitted. May the history of the real deeds of an inspired heroine bring some hours of elevated pleasure to many a home.

O. W. WIGHT.

Brooklyn, Sept., 1858.

MAID OF ORLEANS.

THE originality of the Pucelle, the secret of her success, was not her courage or her visions, but her good sense. Amidst all her enthusiasm, the girl of the people clearly saw the question, and knew how to resolve it. The knot which politician and doubter could not unloose, she cut. She pronounced, in God's name, Charles VII. to be the heir: she reässured him as to his legitimacy, of which he had doubts himself; and she sanctified this legitimacy by taking him straight to Reims, and, by her quickness, gaining over the English the decisive advantage of the coronation.

It was by no means rare to see women take up arms. They often fought in sieges: witness the eighty women wounded at Amiens: witness Jeanne Hachette. In the Pucelle's day, and in the self-same years as she, the Bohemian women fought like men in the wars of the Hussites.

No more, I repeat, did the originality of the Pucelle consist in her visions. Who but had visions in the middle age? Even in this prosaic fifteenth century, excess of suffering had singularly exalted men's imaginations. We find at Paris, one brother Richard, so exciting the populace by his sermons, that at last the English banished him the city. Assemblies of from fifteen to twenty thousand souls were collected by the preaching of the Breton Carmelite friar, Conecta, at Courtrai and at Arras. In the space of a few years, before and after the Pucelle, every province had its saint — either a Pierrette, a Breton peasant girl who holds converse with Jesus Christ; or a Marie of Avignon, a Catherine of Rochelle; or a poor shepherd, such as Saintrailles brings up from his own country, who has the stigmata on his feet and hands, and who sweats blood on holy days, like the present holy woman of the Tyrol.

Lorraine, apparently, was one of the last provinces to expect such a phenomenon from. The Lorrainers are brave, and apt to blows, but most delight in stratagem and craft. If the great Guise saved France, before disturbing her, it was not by visions. Two Lorrainers make themselves conspicuous at the siege of Orléans, and both display the natural humor of their witty countryman, Callot; one of these is the cannonier, master Jean, who used to counterfeit death so well; the other is a knight who, being taken by the English and loaded with chains, when they withdrew, returned riding on the back of an English monk.

The character of the Lorraine of the Vosges, it is true, is of graver kind. This lofty district, from whose mountain sides rivers run seaward through France in every direction, was covered with forests of such vast size as to be esteemed by the Carlovingians the most worthy of their imperial hunting parties. In glades of these forests rose the venerable abbeys of Luxeuil and Remiremont; the latter, as is well known, under the rule of an abbess who was ever a princess of the Holy Empire, who had her great officers, in fine, a whole feudal court, and used to be preceded by her seneschal, bearing the naked sword. The dukes of Lorraine had been vassals, and for a long period, of this female sovereignty.

It was precisely between the Lorraine of the Vosges and that of the plains, between Lorraine and Champagne, at Dom-Remy, that the brave and beautiful girl, destined to bear so well the sword of France, first saw the light.

Along the Meuse, and within a circuit of ten leagues, there are four Dom-Remys; three in the diocese of Toul, one in that of Langres. It is probable that these four villages were, in ancient times, dependencies of the abbey of Saint-Remy, at Reims. In the Carlovingian period, our great abbeys are known to have held much more distant possessions; as far, indeed, as in Provence, in Germany, and even in England.

This line of the Meuse is the *march* of Lorraine and of Champagne, so long an object of contention betwixt monarch and duke. Jeanne's father, Jacques Darc, was a worthy Champenois. Jeanne, no doubt, inherited her disposition from this parent; she had none of the Lorraine ruggedness, but much rather the Champenois mildness; that simplicity, blended with sense and shrewdness, which is observable in Joinville.

A few centuries earlier, Jeanne would have been born the serf of the abbey of Saint-Remy; a century earlier, the serf of the sire de Joinville, who was lord of Vaucouleurs, on which city the village of Dom-Remy depended. But, in 1335, the king obliged the Joinvilles to cede Vaucouleurs to him. It formed at that time the grand channel of communication between

Champagne and Lorraine, and was the high road to Germany, as well as that of the bank of the Meuse — the cross or intersecting point of the two routes. It was, too, we may say, the frontier between the two great parties: near Dom-Remy was one of the last villages that held to the Burgundians; all the rest was for Charles VII.

In all ages this *march* of Lorraine and of Champagne had suffered cruelly from war; first, a long war between the east and the west, between the king and the duke, for the possession of Neufchâteau and the adjoining places; then war between the north and south, between the Burgundians and the Armagnacs. The remembrance of these pitiless wars has never been effaced. Not long since was seen, near Neufchâteau, an antique tree with sinister name, whose branches had no doubt often borne human fruit — *Chêne des Partisans*, (the Partisans' Oak.)

The poor people of the *march* had the honor of being directly subject to the king; that is, in reality, they belonged to no one, were neither supported nor managed by any one, and had no lord or protector but God. People so situated are of a serious cast. They know that they can count upon nothing; neither on their goods nor on their lives. They sow, the soldier reaps. Nowhere does the husbandman feel greater anxiety about the affairs of his country, none have a directer interest in them; the least reverse shakes him so roughly! He inquires, he strives to know and to forsee; above all, he is resigned; whatever happens, he is prepared for it; he is patient and brave. Women even become so; they must become so, among all these soldiers, if not for the sake of life, for that of honor, like Goëthe's beautiful and hardy Dorothea.

Jeanne was the third daughter of a laborer,* Jacques *Darc,* and of Isabella *Romée.*† Her two godmothers were called, the one, *Jeanne,* the other, *Sibylle.*

Their eldest son had been named *Jacques,* and another, *Pierre.* The

---

* There may be seen at this day, above the door of the hut where Jeanne Darc lived, three scutcheons carved on stone — that of Louis XI., who beautified the hut; that which was undoubtedly given to one of her brothers, along with the surname of Du Lis; and a third, charged with a star and three ploughshares, to image the mission of the Pucelle and the humble condition of her parents. Vallet, Mémoire adressé à l'Institut Historique, sur le nom de famille de la Pucelle.

† The name of *Romee* was often assumed in the middle age by those who had made the pilgrimage to Rome.

2

pious parents gave one of their daughters the loftier name of Saint-*Jean.**

While the other children were taken by their father to work in the fields, or set to watch cattle, the mother kept Jeanne at home, sewing or spinning. She was taught neither reading nor writing; but she learned all her mother knew of sacred things. She imbibed her religion, not as a lesson or a ceremony, but in the popular and simple form of an evening fireside story, as a truth of a mother's telling. . . . What we imbibe thus with our blood and milk, is a living thing, is life itself. . . .

As regards Jeanne's piety, we have the affecting testimony of the friend of her infancy, of her bosom friend, Haumette, who was younger than she

---

* This Christian name is that of a great number of celebrated men of the middle age.

by three or four years. "Over and over again," she said, "I have been at her father's, and have slept with her, in all love (*de bonne amitié*). . . . She was a very good girl, simple and gentle. She was fond of going to church, and to holy places. She spun, and attended to the house, like other girls. . . . She confessed frequently. She blushed when told that she was too devout, and went too often to church." A laborer, also summoned to give evidence, adds, that she nursed the sick, and was charitable to the poor. "I know it well," were his words; "I was then a child, and it was she who nursed me."

Her charity, her piety, were known to all. All saw that she was the best girl in the village. What they did not see and know was, that in her, celestial ever absorbed worldly feelings, and suppressed their development. She had the divine gift to remain, soul and body, a child. She grew up strong and beautiful; but never knew the physical sufferings entailed on woman. They were spared her, that she might be the more devoted to religious thought and inspiration. Born under the very walls of the church, lulled in her cradle by the chimes of the bells, and nourished by legends, she was herself a legend, a quickly passing and pure legend, from birth to death.

She was a living legend . . . but her vital spirits, exalted and concentrated, did not become the less creative. The young girl *created*, so to speak, unconsciously, and *realized* her own ideas, endowing them with being, and imparting to them, out of the strength of her original vitality, such splendid and all-powerful existence, that they threw into the shade the wretched realities of this world.

If poetry mean *creation*, this undoubtedly, is the highest poetry. Let us trace the steps by which she soared thus high from so lowly a starting-point.

Lowly in truth, but already poetic. Her village was close to the vast forests of the Vosges. From the door of her father's house she could see the old *oak* wood, the wood haunted by fairies; whose favorite spot was a fountain near a large beech, called the fairies', or the *ladies*' tree. On this the children used to hang garlands, and would sing around it. These antique *ladies* and mistresses of the woods were, it was said, no longer permitted to assemble round the fountain, barred by their sins. However, the Church was always mistrustful of the old local divinities; and to ensure their complete expulsion, the *curé* annually said a mass at the fountain.

Amidst these legends and popular dreams, Jeanne was born. But, along with these, the land presented a poetry of a far different character, savage, fierce, and, alas! but too real,—the poetry of war. War! all passions and emotions are included in this single word. It is not that every day brings with it assault and plunder, but it brings the fear of them—the tocsin, the awaking with a start, and, in the distant horizen, the lurid light of conflagration, . . . a fearful but poetic state of things. The most prosaic of men, the lowland Scots, amidst the hazards of the *border*, have become poets: in this sinister desert, which even yet looks as if it were a region accursed, ballads, wild but long-lived flowers, have germed and flourished.

Jeanne had her share in these ro-
mantic adventures. She would see
poor fugitives seek refuge in her village, would assist in sheltering them,
give them up her bed, and sleep herself in the loft. Once, too, her parents
had been obliged to turn fugitives; and
then, when the flood of brigands had
swept by, the family returned and
found the village sacked, the house
devastated, the church burnt.

Thus she knew what war was.
Thoroughly did she understand this
anti-Christian state, and unfeigned was
her horror of this reign of the devil,
in which every man died in mortal sin.
She asked herself whether God would
always allow this, whether he would
not prescribe a term to such miseries,
whether he would not send a liberator
as he had so often done for Israel — a
Gideon, a Judith? . . . She knew

that woman had more than once saved God's own people, and that from the beginning it had been foretold that woman should bruise the serpent. No doubt she had seen over the portal of the churches St. Margaret, together with St. Michael, trampling under foot the dragon. . . . If, as all the world said, the ruin of the kingdom was a woman's work, an unnatural mother's, its redemption might well be a virgin's: and this, moreover, had been foretold in a prophecy of Merlin's; a prophecy which, embellished and modified by the habits of each province, had become altogether Lorraine in Jeanne Darc's country. According to the prophecy current here, it was a Pucelle of the marches of *Lorraine* who was to save the realm; and the prophecy had probably assumed this form through the recent marriage of Réné of Anjou with the heiress of the duchy of Lorraine, a marriage which, in truth, turned out very happily for the kingdom of France.

One summer's day, a fast-day, Jeanne being at noontide in her father's garden, close to the church, saw a dazzling light on that side, and heard a voice say, "Jeanne, be a good and obedient child, go often to church." The poor girl was exceedingly alarmed.

Another time she again heard the voice and saw the radiance; and, in the midst of the effulgence, noble figures, one of which had wings, and seemed a wise *prud'homme.* "Jeanne," said this figure to her, "go to the succor of the king of France, and thou shalt restore his kingdom to him." She replied, all trembling, "Messire, I am only a poor girl; I know not how to ride or lead men-at-arms." The voice replied, "Go to M. de Baudricourt, captain of Vaucouleurs, and he will conduct theé to the king. St. Catherine and St. Marguerite will be thy aids." She remained stupified and in tears, as if her whole destiny had been revealed to her.

The *prud'homme* was no less than St. Michael, the severe archangel of judgments, and of battles. He reappeared to her, inspired her with courage, and told her "the pity for the kingdom of France." Then appeared sainted women, all in white, with countless lights around, rich crowns on their heads, and their voices soft and moving unto tears: but Jeanne shed them much more copiously when saints and angels left her. "I longed," she said, "for the angels to take me away too."

If, in the midst of happiness like this she wept, her tears were not causeless.

Bright and glorious as these visions were, a change had from that moment come over her life. She who had hitherto heard but one voice, that of her mother, of which her own was the echo, now heard the powerful voice of angels—and what sought the heavenly voice! That she should quit that mother, quit her dear home. She, whom but a word put out of countenance, was required to mix with men, to address soldiers. She was obliged to quit for the world and for war, her little garden under the shadow of the church, where she heard no ruder sounds than those of its bells, and where the birds ate out of her hand: for such was the attractive sweetness of the young saint, that animals and the fowls of the air came to her, as formerly to the fathers of the desert, in all the trust of God's peace.

Jeanne has told us nothing of this first struggle that she had to undergo: but it is clear that it did take place, and that it was of long duration, since five years elapsed between her first vision, and her final abandonment of her home.

The two authorities, the paternal and the celestial, enjoined her two opposite commands. The one ordered her to remain obscure, modest, and laboring; the other to set out and save the kingdom. The angel bade her arm herself. Her father, rough and honest peasant as he was, swore that rather than his daughter should go away with men-at-arms, he would drown her with his own hands. One or other, disobey she must. Beyond a doubt this was the greatest battle she was called upon to fight; those against the English were play in comparison.

In her family, she encountered not only resistance but temptation; for they attempted to marry her, in the hope of winning her back to more rational notions, as they considered. A young villager pretended that in her childhood she had promised to marry him; and on her denying this, he cited her before the ecclesiastical Judge of Toul. It was imagined that rather than undertake the effort of speaking in her own defence, she would submit to marriage. To the great astonishment of all who knew her, she went to Toul, appeared in court, and spoke — she who had been noted for her modest silence.

In order to escape from the authority of her family, it behooved her to find in the bosom of that family some one who would believe in her: this was the most difficult part of all. In default of her father, she made her uncle a convertite to the truth of her mission. He took her home with him, as if to attend her aunt who was lying-in. She persuaded him to appeal on her behalf to the sire de Baudricourt, captain of Vaucouleurs. The soldier gave a cool reception to the peasant, and told him that the best thing to be done was " to give her a good whipping," and take her back to her father. She was not discouraged; she would go to him, and forced her uncle to accompany her. This was the decisive moment; she quitted forever her village and family, and embraced her friends, above all, her good little friend, Mengette, whom she recommended to God's keeping; as to her elder friend and companion, Haumette, her whom she loved most of all, she preferred quitting without leave-taking.

At length she reached this city of Vaucouleurs, attired in her coarse red peasant's dress, and took up her lodging with her uncle at the house of a wheelwright, whose wife conceived a friendship for her. She got herself taken to Baudricourt, and said to him in a firm tone, "That she came to him from her Lord, to the end that he might send the dauphin word to keep firm, and to fix no day of battle with the enemy, for his Lord would send him succor in Mid-Lent. . . . The realm was not the dauphin's but her Lord's; nevertheless, her Lord willed the dauphin to be king, and to hold the realm in trust." She added, that despite the dauphin's enemies, he would be king, and that she would take him to be crowned.

The captain was much astonished: he suspected that the devil must have a hand in the matter. Thereupon, he consulted the *curé*, who, apparently, partook his doubts. She had not spoken of her visions to any priest or churchman. So the *curé* accompanied the captain to the wheelwright's house, showed his stole, and adjured Jeanne to depart if sent by the evil spirit.

But the people had no doubts; they were struck with admiration. From all sides, crowds flocked to see her. A gentleman, to try her, said to her, "Well, sweetheart; after all, the king will be driven out of the kingdom, and we must turn English." She complained to him of Baudricourt's refusal to take her to the dauphin; "And yet," she said, "before Mid-Lent, I must be with the king, even were I to wear out my legs to the knees; for no one in the world, nor kings, nor dukes, nor daughter of the king of Scotland, can recover the kingdom of France, and he has no other who can succor him save myself, albeit I would prefer staying and spinning with my poor mother, but this is no work of my own; I must go and do it, for it is my Lord's will."—"And who is your lord?"—"God!" . . . The gentleman was touched. He pledged her " his faith, his hand placed in hers, that, with God's guiding, he would conduct her to the king." A young man, of gentle birth, felt himself touched likewise; and declared that he would follow this holy maid.

It appears that Baudricourt sent to ask the king's pleasure; and that in the interim he took Jeanne to see the duke of Lorraine, who was ill, and desired to consult her. All that the duke got from her was advice to appease God by reconciling himself with his wife. Nevertheless, he gave her encouragement.

2

On returning to Vaucouleurs she found there a messenger from the king, who authorized her to repair to court. The reverse of the battle of herrings had determined his counsellors to try any and every means. Jeanne had proclaimed the battle and its result on the very day it was fought; and the people of Vaucouleurs, no longer doubting her mission, subscribed to equip her and buy her a horse. Baudricourt only gave her a sword.

At this moment an obstacle arose. Her parents, informed of her approaching departure, nearly lost their senses, and make the strongest efforts to retain her, commanding, threatening. She withstood this last trial; and got a letter written to them, beseeching them to forgive her.

The journey she was about to undertake was a rough and a most dangerous one. The whole country was over-run by the men-at-arms of both parties. There was neither road, nor bridge, and the rivers were swollen: it was the month of February, 1429.

To travel at such a time with five or six men-at-arms was enough to alarm a young girl. An English woman, or a German, would never have risked such a step; the *indelicacy* of the proceeding would have horrified her. Jeanne was nothing moved by it; she was too pure to entertain any fears of the kind. She wore a man's dress, a dress she wore to the last: this close, and closely fastened dress was her best safeguard. Yet was she young and beautiful. But there was around her, even to those who were most with her, a barrier raised by religion and fear. The youngest of the gentlemen who formed her escort, deposes that though sleeping near her, the shadow of an impure thought never crossed his mind.

She traversed with heroic serenity these districts, either desert, or infested with soldiers. Her companions regretted having set out with her, some of them thinking that she might be perhaps a witch; and they felt a strong desire to abandon her. For herself, she was so tranquil, that she would stop at every town to hear mass. "Fear nothing," she said, "God guides me my way; 'tis for this I was born." And again, "My brothers in paradise tell me what I am to do."

Charles VIIth's court was far from being unanimous in favor of the Pucelle. This inspired maid, coming from Lorraine, and encouraged by the duke of Lorraine, could not fail to strengthen the queen's and her mother's party, the party of Lorraine and of Anjou, with the king. An ambuscade was laid for the Pucelle some distance from Chinon, and it was a miracle she escaped.

So strong was the opposition to her, that when she arrived, the question of her being admitted to the king's presence was debated for two days in the council. Her enemies hoped to adjourn the matter indefinitely, by proposing that an inquiry should be instituted concerning her in her native place. Fortunately, she had friends as well, the two queens, we may be assured, and, especially, the duke of Alençon, who having recently left English keeping, was impatient to carry the war into the north in order to recover his duchy. The men of Orleans, to whom Dunois had been promising this heavenly aid ever since the 12th of February, sent to the king and claimed the Pucelle.

At last the king received her, and surrounded by all the splendor of his court, in the hope, apparently, of disconcerting her. It was evening; the light of fifty torches illumed the hall, and a brilliant array of nobles and above three hundred knights were assembled round the monarch. Every one was curious to see the sorceress, or, as it might be, the inspired maid.

The sorceress was eighteen years of age; she was a beautiful and most desirable girl, of good height, and with a sweet and heart-touching voice.

She entered the splendid circle with all humility "like a poor little shepherdess," distinguished at the first glance the king, who had purposely kept himself amidst the crowd of courtiers, and although at first he maintained that he was not the king, she fell down and embraced his knees. But as he had not been crowned, she only styled him dauphin :—"Gentle dauphin," she addressed him, "my name is Jehanne la Pucelle. The King of heaven sends you word by me that you shall be consecrated and crowned in the city of Rheims, and shall be lieutenant of the King of heaven, who is king of France." The king then took her aside, and, after a moment's consideration, both changed countenance. She told him, as she subsequently acknowledged to her confessors :—"I am commissioned by my Lord to tell you, that you are the *true heir* to the French throne, and the *king's son.*" *

* According to a somewhat later, but still very probable account, she reminded him of a circumstance known to himself alone; namely, that one morning in his oratory he had prayed to God to restore his kingdom to him *if he were the lawful heir,* but that if he were not, that He would grant him the mercy not to be killed or thrown into prison, but

A circumstance which awoke still greater astonishment and a sort of fear is, that the first prediction which fell from her lips was accomplished the instant it was made. A soldier who was struck by her beauty, and who expressed his desires aloud with the coarseness of the camp, and swearing by his God: "Alas!" she exclaimed, "thou deniest him, and art so near thy death!" A moment after, he fell into the river and was drowned.

Her enemies started the objection, that if she knew the future it must be through the devil. Four or five bishops were got together to examine her; but through fear, no doubt, of compromising themselves with either of the parties which divided the court, they

to be able to take refuge in Spain or in Scotland. — Sala, Exemples de Hardiesse, MS. Français, de la Bibl. Royale, No. 180.

referred the examination to the University of Poitiers, in which great city was both university, parliament, and a number of able men.

The archbishop of Rheims, chancellor of France, president of the royal council, issued his mandate to the doctors, and to the professors of theology — the one priests, the others monks, and charged them to examine the Pucelle.

The doctors introduced, and placed in a hall, the young maid seated herself at the end of the bench, and replied· to their questionings. She related with a simplicity that rose to grandeur the apparitions of angels with which she had been visited, and their words. A single objection was raised by a Dominican, but it was a serious one — "Jehanne, thou sayest that God wishes to deliver the people of France; if such be his will, he has no need of men-at-arms." She was not disconcerted:—"Ah! my God," was her reply, "the men-at-arms will fight, and God will give the victory."

Another was more difficult to be satisfied—a Limousin, brother Seguin, professor of theology at the university of Poitiers, a "very sour man," says the chronicle. He asked her in his Limousin French, what tongue that pretended celestial voice spoke? Jehanne answered, a little too hastily, "A better than yours."—"Dost thou believe in God?" said the doctor, in a rage: "Now, God wills us not to have faith in thy words, except thou showest a sign." She replied, "I have not come to Poitiers to show signs or work miracles; my sign will be the raising of the siege of Orleans. Give me men-at-arms, few or many, and I will go."

Meanwhile, it happened at Poitiers as at Vaucouleurs, her sanctity seized the hearts of the people. In a moment, all were for her. Women, ladies, citizens' wives, all flocked to see her at the house where she was staying, with the wife of an advocate to the parliament, and all returned full of emotion. Men went there too; and counsellors, advocates, old hardened judges, who had suffered themselves to be taken thither incredulously, when they had heard her, wept even as the women did, and said, "The maid is of God."

The examiners themselves went to see her, with the king's equerry; and on their recommencing their never-ending examination, quoting learnedly to her, and proving to her from the writings of all the doctors that she ought not to be believed, "Hearken," she said to them, "there is more in God's book than in yours. . . . I know neither A nor B; but I come commissioned by God to raise the siege of Orléans, and to have the dauphin crowned at Rheims. . . . First, however, I must write to the English, and summon them to depart; God will have it so. Have you paper and ink? Write as I dictate. . . . To you! Suffort, Classidas, and La Poule, I summon you, on the part of the King of heaven, to depart to England." . . . They wrote as she dictated; she had won over her very judges.

They pronounced as their opinion, that it was lawful to have recourse to the young maiden. The archbishop of Embrun, who had been consulted, pronounced similarly; supporting his opinion by showing how God had frequently revealed to virgins, for instance, to the sibyls, what he concealed from men; how the demon could not make a covenant with a virgin; and recommending it to be ascertained whether Jehanne were a virgin. Thus, being pushed to extremity, and either not being able or being unwilling to explain the delicate distinction betwixt good and evil revelations, knowledge humbly referred a ghostly matter to a corporeal test, and made this grave question of the spirit depend on woman's mystery.

As the doctors could not decide, the ladies did; and the honor of the Pucelle was vindicated by a jury, with the good queen of Sicily, the king's mother-in-law, at their head. This farce over; and some Franciscans who had been deputed to inquire into Jehanne's character in her own country bringing the most favorable report, there was no time to lose. Orléans was crying out for succor, and Dunois sent entreaty upon entreaty. The Pucelle was equipped, and a kind of establishment arranged for her. For squire she had a brave knight, of mature years, Jean Daulon, one of Dunois's household, and of its best conducted and most discreet members. She had, also, a noble page, two heralds-at-arms, a *maître d'hôtel*, and two valets: her brother, Pierre Darc, too, was one of her attendants. Jean Pasquerel, a brother eremite of the order of St. Augustin, was given her for confessor. Generally speaking, the monks, particularly the mendicants, were staunch supporters of this marvel of inspiration.

And it was, in truth, for those who beheld the sight, a marvel to see for the first time Jehanne Darc in her white armor and on her beautiful black horse, at her side a small axe, and the sword of Saint-Catherine, which sword had been discovered, on her intimation, behind the altar of Saint-Catherine-de-Fierbois. In her hand she bore a white standard, embroidered with fleurs-de-lis, and on which God was represented with the world in his hands, having on his right and left two angels, each holding a fleur-de-lis. " I will not," she said, " use my sword to slay any one ;" and she added, that although she loved her sword, she loved " forty times more " her standard. Let us contrast the two parties, at the moment of her departure for Orléans.

The English had been much reduced by their long winter siege. After Salisbury's death, many men-at-arms whom he, had engaged, thought themselves relieved from their engagements and departed. The Burgundians, too, had been recalled by their duke. When the most important of the English bastilles was forced, into which the defenders of some other bastilles had thrown themselves, only five hundred men were found in it. In all, the English force may have amounted to two or three thousand men; and of this small number part were French, and, no doubt, not to be much depended upon by the English.

Collected together, they would have constituted a respectable force; but they were distributed among a dozen bastilles or boulevards, between which there was, for the most part, no communication; a disposition of their forces, which proves that Talbot and the other English leaders had hitherto been rather brave and lucky than intelligent and skilful. It was evident that each of these small isolated forts would be weak against the large city which they pretended to hold in check; that its numerous population, rendered warlike by a siege, would at last besiege the besiegers.

On reading the formidable list of the captains who threw themselves into Orléans, La Hire, Saintrailles, Gaucourt, Culan, Coaraze, Armagnac; and remembering that, independently of the Bretons under Marshal de Retz, and the Gascons under Marshal de St. Sévère — the captain of Châteaudun, Florent d'Illiers, had brought all the nobility of the neighborhood with him to this short expedition, the deliverance of Orleans seems less miraculous.

It must, however, be acknowledged that for this great force to act with efficiency, the one essential and indis-

pensable requisite, unity of action, was
wanting. Had skill and intelligence
sufficed to impart it, the want would
have been supplied by Dunois; but
there was something more required —
authority, and more than royal authority, too, for the king's captains were
little in the habit of obeying the king:
to subject these savage, untamable
spirits, God's authority was called for.
Now, the God of this age was the Virgin much more than Christ; and it behooved that the Virgin should descend
upon earth, be a popular Virgin, young,
beauteous, gentle, bold.

War had changed men into wild
beasts; these beasts had to be restored
to human shape, and be converted into
docile Christian men — a great and a
hard change. Some of these Armagnac captains were, perhaps, the most
ferocious mortals that ever existed;

as may be inferred from the name of but one of. them, a name that strikes terror, Gilles de Retz, the original of Blue Beard. ·

One hold, however, was left upon their souls; they had cast off humanity and nature, without having been able wholly to disengage themselves from religion. These brigands, it is true, hit upon strange means of reconciling religion and robbery. One of them, the Gascon La Hire, gave vent to the original remark, "Were God to turn man-at-arms, he would be a plunderer;" and when he went on a foray, he offered up his little Gascon prayer without entering too minutely into his wants, conceiving that God would take a hint — "Sire God, I pray thee to do for La Hire what La Hire would do for thee, wert thou a captain, and were La Hire God." *

* "Sire Dieu, je te prie de faire pour la Hire ce

It was at once a risible and a touching sight to see the sudden conversion of the old Armagnac brigands. They did not reform by halves. La Hire durst no longer swear; and the Pucelle took compassion on the violence he did himself, and allowed him to swear "by his baton." The devils found themselves all of a sudden turned into little saints.

The Pucelle had begun by requiring them to give up their mistresses, and attend to confession. Next, on their march along the Loire, she had an altar raised in the open air, at which she partook of the communion, and they as well. The beauty of the season, the charm of a spring in Touraine, must have added singularly to the re-

que La Hire ferait pour toi, si tu étais capitaine et si La Hire était Dieu." Mémoires concernant la Pucelle, Collection Petitot, viii. 127.

ligious supremacy of the young maid. They themselves had grown young again, had utterly forgotten what they were, and felt, as in the spring-time of life, full of good-will and of hope, all young like her, all children. . . . With her they commenced, and unreservedly, a new life. Where was she leading them? Little did it matter to them. They would have followed her, not to Orléans only, but just as readily to Jerusalem. And the English were welcome to go thither too: in a letter she addressed to them she graciously proposed that they all, French and English, should unite, and proceed conjointly to deliver the Holy Sepulchre.

The first night of encamping she lay down all armed, having no females with her; and, not being yet accustomed to the hardships of such a mode of life, felt indisposed the next day. As to danger, she knew not what it meant. She wanted to cross the river, and advance on the northern or English side, right among their bastilles, asserting that the enemy would not budge; but the captains would not listen to her, and they followed the other bank, crossing two leagues below Orléans. Dunois came to meet her: "I bring you," she said, "the best succor mortal ever received, that of the King of heaven. It is no succor of mine, but from God himself, who, at the prayer of St. Louis and St. Charlemagne, has taken pity on the town of Orléans, and will not allow the enemy to have at one and the same time the duke's body and his city.

She entered the city at eight o'clock of the evening of April 29th, and so great and so eager was the crowd, striving to touch her horse at least, that her progress through the streets was exceedingly slow; they gazed at her "as if they were beholding God."* She rode along speaking kindly to the people, and, after offering up prayers in the church, repaired to the house of the Duke of Orléans' treasurer; an honorable man, whose wife and daughters gladly welcomed her; she slept with Charlotte one of the daughters.

She had entered the city with the supplies; but the main body of the relieving force fell down as far as Blois, where it crossed the river. Nevertheless, she was eager for an immediate attack on the English bas-

---

* She seemed, at the least, an angel, a creature above all physical wants. At times, she would continue a whole day on horseback, without alighting, eating, or drinking, and would only take in the evening some sippets of bread in wine and water. See the evidence of the various witnesses, and the Chronique de la Pucelle, éd. Buchon (1827), p. 309.

tilles, and would summon the northern bastilles to surrender, a summons which she repeated, and then proceeded to summon the southern bastilles. Here Glasdale overwhelmed her with abuse, calling her cow-herd and prostitute (*vachère et ribaude.*) In reality, they believed her to be a sorceress, and felt great terror of her. They detained her herald-at-arms, and were minded to burn him, in the hope that it would break the charm; but, first, they considered it advisable to consult the doctors of the university of Paris. Besides, Dunois threatened to retaliate on their herald whom he had in his power. As to the Pucelle, she had no fears for her herald, but sent another, saying, " Go, tell Talbot if he will appear in arms, so will I. . . . if he can take me, let him burn me."

The army delaying, Dunois ventured

to sally forth in search of it; and the Pucelle, left behind, found herself absolute mistress of the city, where all authority but hers seemed to be at an end. She caracolled round the walls, and the people followed her fearlessly. The next day, she rode out to reconnoitre the English bastilles, and young women and children went, too, to look at these famous bastilles, where all remained still, and betrayed no sign of movement. She led back the crowd with her to attend vespers at the church of Saint-Croix; and as she wept at prayers, they all wept likewise. The citizens were beside themselves; they were raised above all fears, were drunk with religion and with war,—seized by one of those formidable accesses of fanaticism in which men can do all, and believe all, and in which they are scarcely less terrible to friends than to enemies.

Charles VIIth's chancellor, the arch-bishop of Rheims, had detained the small army at Blois. The old politician was far from imagining such re-sistless enthusiasm, or, perhaps, he dreaded it. So he repaired to Orléans with great unwillingness. The Pu-celle, followed by the citizens and priests singing hymns, went to meet him, and the whole procession passed and repassed the English bastilles. The army entered, protected by priests and a girl.

This girl, who, with all her enthusi-asm and inspiration, had great pene-tration, was quickly aware of the cold malevolence of the new-comers, and perceived that they wanted to do with-out her, at the risk of ruining all. Dunois having owned to her that he feared the enemy's being reinforced by the arrival of fresh troops under Sir John Falstaff, "Bastard, bastard," she said to him, "in God's name I command thee as soon as you know of his coming to apprize me of it, for if he passes without my knowledge, I promise you that I will take off your head."

She was right in supposing that they wished to do without her. As she was snatching a moment's rest with her young bedfellow, Charlotte, she suddenly starts up, and exclaims, "Great God, the blood of our countrymen is running on the ground. . . . 'tis ill done! why did they not awake me? Quick, my arms, my horse!" She was armed in a moment, and finding her young page playing below, "Cruel boy," she said to him, "not to tell me that the blood of France was spilling."

She set off at a gallop, and coming upon the wounded who were being brought in, "Never," she exclaimed, "have I seen a Frenchman's blood without my hair rising up!"

On her arrival, the flying rallied. Dunois, who had not been apprized any more than she, came up at the same time. The bastille (one of the northern bastilles) was once more attacked. Talbot endeavored to cover it; but fresh troops sallying out of Orléans, the Pucelle put herself at their head, Talbot drew off his men, and the fort was carried.

Many of the English who had put on the priestly habit by way of protection were brought in by the Pucelle, and placed in her own house to ensure their safety; she knew the ferocity of her followers. It was her first victory, the first time she had ever seen a field of carnage. She wept on seeing so many human beings who had perished unconfessed. She desired the benefit of confession for herself and retainers, and as the next day was Ascension Day, declared her intention of communicating and of passing the day in prayer.

They took advantage of this to hold a council without her; at which it was determined to cross the Loire and attack St. Jean-le-Blanc, the bastille which most obstructed the introduction of supplies, making at the same time a false attack on the side of La Beauce. The Pucelle's enviers told her of the false attack only; but Dunois apprised her of the truth.

The English then did what they ought to have done before: they concentrated their strength. Burning down the bastille, which was the ob-

ject of the intended attack, they fell
back on the two other bastilles on the
south — the Augustins' and the Tournelles: but the Augustins' was at once
attacked and carried. This success,
again, was partly due to the Pucelle;
for the French being seized with a
panic terror, and retreating precipi-
tately towards the floating bridge
which had been thrown over the river,
the Pucelle and La Hire disengaged
themselves from the crowd, and, crossing in boats, took the English in flank.

There remained the Tournelles, before which bastille the conquerers
passed the night; but they constrained
the Pucelle, who had not broken her
fast the whole day (it was Friday,) to
recross the Loire. Meanwhile the
council assembled: and in the evening it was announced to the Pucelle
that they had unanimously determined,

as the city was now well victualled, to wait for reinforcements before attacking the Tournelles. It is difficult to suppose such to have been the serious intention of the chiefs; the English momentarily expecting the arrival of Sir John Falstoff with fresh troops, all delay was dangerous. Probably the object was to deceive the Pucelle, and to deprive her of the honor of the success to which she had largely prepared the way. But she was not to be caught in the snare.

"You have been at your council," she said, "I have been at mine;" then, turning to her chaplain, "come to-morrow at break of day, and quit me not; I shall have much to do — blood will go out of my body; I shall be wounded below my bosom."

In the morning, her host endeavored te detain her. "Stay, Jeanne," he

said, "let us partake together of this
fish which is just fresh caught."
"Keep it," she answered gayly, "keep
it till night, when I shall come back
over the bridge, after having taken
the Tournelles, and I will bring you a
godden to eat of it with us." *

Then she hurried forward with a
number of men-at-arms and of citizens
to the *porte de Bourgogne;* which she
found kept closed by the sire de Gaucourt, grand master of the king's
household. "You are a wicked man,"
said Jeanne to him; "but whether you
will or not, the men-at-arms shall pass."
Gaucourt felt that with this excited

---

* "The witness Colette deposed that Godon
[Godden?] was a nickname for the English, taken
from their common exclamation of 'God damn it,'
so that this vulgarity was a national characteristic
in the reign of Henry VI."—Note, p. 78, vol. iii.,
Turner's Hist. of England.

multitude his life hung by a thread; and besides, his own followers would not obey him. The crowd opened the gate, and forced another which was close to it.

The sun was rising upon the Loire at the very moment this multitude were throwing themselves into boats. However, when they reached the Tournelles, they found their want of artillery, and sent for it into the town. At last they attacked the redoubt which covered the bastille. The English made a brave defence. Perceiving that the assailants began to slacken in their efforts, the Pucelle threw herself into the fosse, seized a ladder, and was rearing it against the wall, when she was struck by an arrow betwixt her neck and shoulder. The English rushed out to make her prisoner, but she was borne off. Removed from the scene

5

of conflict, laid on the grass, and disarmed, when she saw how deep the wound was — the arrow's point came out behind — she was terrified, and burst into tears. Suddenly she rises; her holy ones had appeared to her; she repels the men-at-arms, who were for *charming* the wound by words, protesting that she would not be cured contrary to the Divine will. She only allowed a dressing of oil to be applied to the wound, and then confessed herself.

Meanwhile no progress was made, and it was near nightfall. Dunois himself ordered the retreat to be sounded. " Rest awhile," she said, " eat and drink; " and she betook herself to prayers in a vineyard. A Basque soldier had taken from the hands of the Pucelle's squire her banner, that banner so dreaded by the enemy: " As soon as the standard shall touch the wall," she exclaimed, "you can enter."—"It touches it."—"Then enter, all is yours." And, in fact, the assailants, transported beyond themselves, mounted "as if at a bound." The English were at this moment attacked on both sides at once.

For the citizens of Orléans, who had eagerly watched the struggle from the other side of the Loire, could no longer contain themselves, but opened their gates and rushed upon the bridge. One of the arches being broken, they threw over it a sorry plank; and a knight of St. John, completely armed, was the first to venture across. At last, the bridge was repaired after a fashion, and the crowd flowed over. The English, seeing this sea of people rushing on, thought that the whole world was got together. Their imaginations grew excited: some saw St. Aignan, the patron of the city; others the Archangel Michael fighting on the French side. As Glasdale was about to retreat from the redoubt into the bastille, across a small bridge which connected the two, the bridge was shivered by a cannon-ball, and he was precipitated into the water below, and drowned before the eyes of the Pucelle, whom he had so coarsely abused. "Ah!" she exclaimed, "how I pity thy soul." There were five hundred men in the bastille: they were all put to the sword.

Not an Englishman remained to the south of the Loire. On the next day, Sunday, those who were on the north side abandoned their bastilles, their artillery, their prisoners, their sick. Talbot and Suffolk directed the retreat, which was made in good order, and with a bold front. The Pucelle forbade pursuit, as they retired of their own accord. But before they had lost sight of the city, she ordered an altar to be raised in the plain, had mass sung, and the Orléanois returned thanks to God in presence of the enemy (Sunday, May 8).

The effect produced by the deliverance of Orléans was beyond calculation. All recognized it to be the work of a supernatural power; which though some ascribed to the devil's agency, most referred to God, and it began to be the general impression that Charles VII. had right on his side.

Six days after the raising of the siege, Gerson published a discourse to prove that this marvellous event might be reasonably considered God's own doing. The good Christine de Pisan also wrote to congratulate her sex;

and many treatises were published, more favorable than hostile to the Pucelle, and even by subjects of the Duke of Burgundy, the ally of the English.

CORONATION OF CHARLES VII.

Charles VIIth's policy was to seize the opportunity, march boldly from Orléans to Rheims, and lay hand on the crown — seemingly a rash, but in reality a safe step, before the English had recovered from their panic. Since they had committed the capital blunder of not having yet crowned their young Henry VI., it behooved to be beforehand with them. He who was first anointed king would remain king. It would also be a great thing for Charles VII. to make his royal progress through English France, to take possession, to show that in every part of France the king was at home.

Such was the counsel of the Pucelle alone, and this heroic folly was consummate wisdom. The politic and shrewd among the royal counsellors, those whose judgment was held in most esteem, smiled at the idea, and recommended proceeding slowly and surely: in other words, giving the English time to recover their spirits. They all, too, had an interest of their own in the advice they gave. The Duke of Alençon recommended marching into Normandy — with a view to the recovery of Alençon. Others, and they were listened to, counselled staying upon the Loire, and reducing the smaller towns. This was the most timid counsel of all; but it was to the interest of the houses of Orléans and of Anjou, and of the Poitevin, La Trémouille, Charles VIIth's favorite.

Suffolk had thrown himself into Jargeau : it was attacked, and carried by assault. Beaugency was next taken, before Talbot could receive the reinforcements sent him by the regent, under the command of Sir John Falstoff. The constable, Richemont, who had long remained secluded in his own domains, came with his Bretons, contrary to the wishes of either the king or the Pucelle, to the aid of the victorious army.

A battle was imminent, and Richemont was come to carry off its honors. Talbot and Falstoff had effected a junction; but, strange to tell, though the circumstance paints to the life the state of the country and the fortuitous nature of the war, no one knew where to find the English army, lost in the desert of La Beauce, the which district was then overrun with thickets and brambles. A stag led to the discovery: chased by the French vanguard, the scared animal rushed into the English ranks.

The English happened to be on their march, and had not, as usual, intrenched themselves behind their stakes. Talbot alone wished to give battle, maddened as he was at having shown his back to the French at Orléans. Sir John Falstoff, on the contrary, who had gained the battle of herrings, did not require to fight to recover his reputation, but with much prudence advised, as the troops were discouraged, remaining on the defensive. The French men-at-arms did not wait for the English leaders to make up their minds, but, coming up at a gallop, encountered but slight resistance. Talbot would fight, seeking, perhaps, to fall; but he only succeeded in getting made prisoner. The pursuit was murderous; and the bodies of two thousand of the English strewed the plain. At the sight of such numbers of dead La Pucelle shed tears; but she wept much more bitterly when she saw the brutality of the soldiery, and how they treated prisoners who had no ransom to give. Perceiving one of them felled, dying, to the ground, she was no longer mistress of herself, but threw herself from her horse, raised the poor man's head, sent for a priest, comforted him, and smoothed his way to death.

After this battle of Patay (June 28 or 29), the hour was come, or never, to hazard the expedition to Rheims. The politic still advised remaining on the Loire; and the securing possession of Cosne and La Charité. This time they spoke in vain; timid voices could no longer gain a hearing. Every day there flocked to the camp men from all the provinces, attracted by the reports of the Pucelle's miracles, believing in her only, and, like her, longing to lead the king to Rheims. There was an irresistible impulse abroad to push forward and drive out the English — the spirit both of pilgrimage and of crusade. The indolent young monarch himself was at last hurried away by this popular tide, which swelled and rolled in northwards. King, courtiers, politicians, enthusiasts, fools, and wise, were off together, either voluntarily or compulsorily. At starting they were twelve thousand; but the mass gathered bulk as it rolled along, fresh comers following fresh comers. They who had no armor joined the holy expedition with no other defence than a leathern jack, as archers or as *coutiliers* (dagsmen), although, may be, of gentle blood.

The army marched from Gien on the 28th of June, and passed before Auxerre without attempting to enter; this city being in the hands of the Duke of Burgundy, whom it was advisable to observe terms with. Troyes was garrisoned partly by Burgundians, partly by English; and they ventured on a sally at the first approach of the royal army. There seemed little hope of forcing so large and well garrisoned a city, and especially without artillery. And how delay, in order to invest it regularly? On the other hand, how advance and leave so strong a place in their rear? Already, too, the army was suffering from want of provisions. Would it not be better to return? The politic were full of triumph at the verification of their forebodings.

There was but one old Armagnac counsellor, the president Maçon, who held the contrary opinion, and who understood that in an enterprise of the kind the wise part was the enthusiastic one, that in a popular crusade reasoning was beside the mark. "When the king undertook this expedition," he argued, " it was not because he had an overwhelming force, or because he had full coffers, or because it was his opinion that the attempt was practicable, but because Jeanne told him to march forward and be crowned at Rheims, and that he would encounter but little opposition, such being God's good pleasure."

Here the Pucelle coming and knocking at the door of the room in which the council was held, assured them that they should enter Troyes in three days. " We would willingly wait six," said the chancellor, " were we certain that you spoke sooth."—"Six! you shall enter to-morrow."

She snatches up her standard; all the troops follow her to the fosse, and they throw into it fagots, doors, tables, rafters, whatever they can lay their hands upon. So quickly was the whole done, that the citizens thought there would soon be no fosses. The English began to lose their head as at Orléans, and fancied they saw a cloud of white butterflies hovering around the magic standard. The citizens, for their part, were filled with alarm, remembering that it was in their city the treaty had been concluded which disinherited Charles VII. They feared being made an example of, took refuge in the two churches, and cried out to surrender. The garrison asked no better, opened a conference, and capitulated on condition of being allowed to march out with what they had.

What they had was, principally, prisoners, Frenchmen. No stipulation on behalf of these unhappy men had been made by Charles's counsellors who drew up the terms of surrender. The Pucelle alone thought of them; and when the English were about to march forth with their manacled prisoners, she stationed herself at the gates, exclaiming, "O my God! they shall not bear them away!" She detained them, and the king paid their ransom.

Master of Troyes on the 9th of July, on the 15th he made his entry into Rheims; and on the 17th (Sunday) he was crowned. That very morning the Pucelle, fulfilling the gospel command to seek reconciliation before offering sacrifice, dictated a beautiful letter to the Duke of Burgundy; without recalling any thing painful, without irritating, without humiliating any one, she said to him with infinite tact and nobleness — " Forgive one another heartily, as good Christians ought to do."

Charles VII. was anointed by the archbishop with oil out of the holy ampulla, brought from Saint-Remy's. Conformably with the antique ritual, he was installed on his throne by the spiritual peers, and served by lay peers both during the ceremony of the coronation and the banquet which followed. Then he went to St. Marculph's to touch for the king's evil. All ceremonies thus duly observed, without the omission of a single particular, Charles was at length, according to the belief of the time, the true and the only king. The English might now crown Henry; but in the estimation of the people, this new coronation would only be a parody of the other.

At the moment the crown was placed on Charles's head, the Pucelle threw herself on her knees, and embraced his legs with a flood of tears. All present melted into tears as well.

She is reported to have addressed him as follows:—"O gentle king, now is fulfilled the will of God, who was pleased that I should raise the siege of Orléans, and should bring you to your city of Rheims to be crowned and anointed, showing you to be true king and rightful possessor of the realm of France."

The Pucelle was in the right: she had done and finished what she had to do: and so, amidst the joy of this triumphant solemnity, she entertained the idea, the presentiment, perhaps, of her approaching end. When, on entering

6

Rheims with the king, the citizens came out to meet them singing hymns, "Oh, the worthy, devout people!" she exclaimed, . . . "I If must die, happy should I feel to be buried here." — "Jehanne," said the archbishop to her, "where then do you think you will die?"—"I have no idea; where it shall please God. . . . I wish it would please him that I should go and tend sheep with my sister and my brothers. . . . They would be so happy to see me! . . . At least, I have done what our Lord commanded me to do." And raising her eyes to heaven, she returned thanks. All who saw her at that moment, says the old chronicle, "believed more firmly than ever that she was sent of God."

CARDINAL WINCHESTER.

Such was the virtue of the coronation, and its all-powerful effect in northern France, that from this moment the expedition seemed but to be a peaceable taking of possession, a triumph, a following up of the Rheims festivities. The roads became smooth before the king; the cities opened their gates and lowered their drawbridges. The march was as if a royal pilgrimage from the cathedral of Rheims to St. Medard's, Soissons,—and Notre-Dame, Laon. Stopping for a few days in each city, and then riding on at his pleasure, he made his entry into Château-Thierry, Provins, whence rested and refreshed, he resumed his triumphal progress towards Picardy.

Were there any English left in France?—It might be doubted. Since the battle of Patay, not a word had been heard about Bedford; not that he lacked activity or courage, but

that he had exhausted his last re-
sources. One fact alone will serve to
show the extent of his distress — he
could no longer pay his parliament:
the courts were therefore closed, and
even the entry of the young king
Henry could not be circumstantially
recorded, according to custom, in the
registers, "for want of parchment."

So situated, Bedford could not
choose his means; and he was obliged
to have recourse to the man whom of
all the world he least loved, his uncle,
the rich and all-powerful cardinal Winchester, who, not less avaricious than
ambitious, began haggling about terms,
and speculated upon delay. The
agreement with him was not concluded until the 1st of July, two days
after the defeat of Patay. Charles
VII. then entered Troyes, Rheims —
Paris was in alarm, and Winchester

was still in England. To make Paris
safe, Bedford summoned the Duke of
Burgundy, who came, indeed, but almost alone; and the only advantage
which the regent derived from his
presence was getting him to figure in
an assembly of notables, to speak
therein, and again to recapitulate the
lamentable story of his father's death.
This done, he took his departure;
leaving with Bedford, as all the aid he
could spare, some Picard men-at-arms,
and even exacting, in return, possession of the city of Meaux.

There was no hope but in Winchester. This priest reigned in England.
His nephew, the *Protector*, Gloucester,
the leader of the party of the nobles,
had ruined himself by his imprudence
and follies. From year to year, his
influence at the council table had di-
minished, and Winchester's had in-

creased. He reduced the protector to a cipher, and even managed yearly to pare down the income assigned to the protectorate: this, in a land where each man is strictly valued according to his rental, was murdering him. Winchester, on the contrary, was the wealthiest of the English princes, and one of the great pluralists of the world.   Power follows, as wealth grows.   The cardinal, and the rich bishops of Canterbury, of York, of London, of Ely, and Bath, constituted the council, and if they allowed laymen to sit there, it was only on condition that they should not open their lips: to important sittings, they were not even summoned.   The English government, as might have been foreseen from the moment the house of Lancaster ascended the throne, had become entirely episcopal; a fact evident on the face of the acts passed at this period. In 1429, the chancellor opens the parliament with a tremendous denunciation of heresy; and the council prepares articles against the nobles, whom he accuses of brigandage, and of surrounding themselves with armies of retainers, &c.

In order to raise the cardinal's power to the highest pitch, it required Bedford to be sunk as low in France as Gloucester was in England, that he should be reduced to summon Winchester to his aid, and that the latter, at the head of an army, should come over and crown the young Henry VI. Winchester had the army ready. Having been charged by the pope with a crusade against the Hussites of Bohemia, he had raised, under this pretext, several thousand men. The pope had assigned him, for this object, the money arising from the sale of indulgences; the council of England gave him more money still to detain his levies in France. To the great astonishment of the crusaders they found themselves sold by the cardinal; who was paid twice over for them, paid for an army which served him to make himself king.

With this army, Winchester was to make sure of Paris, and to bring and crown young Henry there. But this coronation could only secure the cardinal's power, in proportion as he should succeed in decrying that of Charles VII., in dishonoring his victories, and ruining him in the minds of the people. Now, he had recourse, as we shall see, to one and the same means (a very efficacious means in that day) against Charles VII. in

France, and against Gloucester in England — a charge of sorcery.

It was not till the 25th of July, nine days after Charles VII. had been well and duly crowned, that the cardinal entered with his army into Paris. Bedford lost not a moment, but put himself in motion with these troops to watch Charles VII. Twice they were in presence, and some skirmishing occurred. Bedford feared for Normandy, and covered it; meanwhile, the king marched upon Paris (August).

This was contrary to the advice of the Pucelle; her voices warned her to go no further than St. Denys. The city of royal burials, like the city of coronations, was a holy city; beyond, she had a presentiment, lay a something over which she would have no power. Charles VII. must have thought so likewise. Was there not danger in bringing this inspiration of warlike sanctity, this poesy of crusade which had so deeply moved the rural districts, face to face with this reasoning, prosaic city, with its sarcastic population, with pedants and Cabochiens?

It was an imprudent step. A city of the kind is not to be carried by a *coup de main;* it is only to be carried by starving it out. But this was out of the question, for the English held the Seine both above and below. They were in force; and were, besides, supported by a considerable number of citizens who had compromised themselves for them. A report, too, was spread that the Armagnacs were coming to destroy the city and raze it to the ground.

Nevertheless, the French carried one

of the outposts. The Pucelle crossed the first fosse, and even cleared the mound which separated it from the second. Arrived at the brink of the latter, she found it full of water; when, regardless of a shower of arrows poured upon her from the city walls, she called for fascines, and began sounding the depth of the water with her lance. Here she stood, almost alone, a mark to all; and, at last, an arrow pierced her thigh. Still, she strove to overcome the pain, and to remain to cheer on the troops to the assault. But loss of blood compelled her to seek the shelter of the first fosse; and it was ten or eleven o'clock at night before she could be persuaded to withdraw to the camp. She seemed to be conscious that this stern check before the walls of Paris must ruin her beyond all hope.

Fifteen hundred men were wounded in this attack, which she was wrongfully accused of having advised. She withdrew, cursed by her own side, by the French, as well as by the English. She had not scrupled to give the assault on the anniversary of the Nativity of Our Lady (September 8th), and the pious city of Paris was exceedingly scandalized thereat.

Still more scandalized was the court of Charles VII. Libertines, the politic, the blind devotees of the letter —sworn enemies of the spirit, all declared stoutly against the spirit, the instant it seemed to fail. The archbishop of Rheims, chancellor of France, who had ever looked but coldly on the Pucelle, insisted, in opposition to her advice, on commencing a negotiation. He himself came to Saint-Denys to propose terms of truce, with, perhaps, a secret hope of gaining over the Duke of Burgundy, at the time at Paris.

Evil regarded and badly supported, the Pucelle laid siege during the winter to Saint-Pierre-le-Moustiers, and la Charité. At the siege of the first, though almost deserted by her men, she persevered in delivering the assault and carried the town. The siege of the second dragged on, languished, and a panic terror dispersed the besiegers.

CAPTURE OF THE PUCELLE.

Meanwhile, the English had persuaded the Duke of Burgundy to aid them in good earnest. The weaker he saw them to be, the stronger was his hope of retaining the places which he might take in Picardy. The English, who had just lost Louviers, placed themselves at his disposal; and the duke, the richest prince in Christendom, no longer hesitated to embark men and money in a war of which he hoped tó reap all the profit. He bribed the governor of Soissons to surrender that city; and then laid siege to Compiègne, the governor of which was, likewise, obnoxious to suspicion. The citizens, however, had compromised themselves too much in the cause of Charles VII. to allow of their town's being betrayed. The Pucelle threw herself into it. On the very same day she headed a sortie, and had nearly surprised the besiegers; but they quickly recovered, and vigorously drove back their assailants as far as the city bridge. The Pucelle, who had remained in the rear to cover the retreat, was too late to enter the gates, either hindered by the crowd that thronged the bridge, or by the sudden shutting of the barriers. She was conspicuous by her dress, and was soon surrounded, seized, and dragged from her horse. Her captor, a Picard archer, — according to others, the bastard of Vendome, — sold her to John of Luxembourg. All, English and Burgundians, saw with astonishment that this object of terror, this monster, this devil, was after all only a girl of eighteen.

That it would end so, she knew beforehand; her cruel fate was inevitable, and — we must say the word — necessary. It was necessary that she should suffer. If she had not gone through her last trial and purification, doubtful shadows would have interposed amidst the rays of glory which rest on that holy figure: she would not have lived in men's minds the MAID OF ORLEANS.

When speaking of raising the siege of Orléans, and of the coronation at Rheims, she had said, "'Tis for this that I was born." These two things accomplished, her sanctity was in peril.

War, sanctity, two contradictory words! Seemingly, sanctity is the direct opposite of war, it is rather love and peace. What young, courageous heart can mingle in battle without participating in the sanguinary intoxication of the struggle and of the victory? . . . On setting out, she had said that she would not use her sword to kill any one. At a later moment she expatiates with pleasure on the sword which she wore at Compiègne, "excellent," as she said, "either for thrusting or cutting." Is not this proof of a change? The saint has become a captain. The Duke of Alençon deposed that she displayed a singular aptitude for the modern arm, the murderous arm, — artillery. The leader of indisciplinable soldiers, and incessantly hurt and aggrieved by their disorders, she became rude and choleric, at least when bent on restraining their excesses. In particular, she was relentless towards the dissolute women who accompanied the camp. One day she struck one of these wretched beings with St. Catherine's sword, with the flat of the sword only; but the virginal weapon, unable to endure the contact, broke, and it could never be reunited.

A short time before her capture, she had herself made prisoner a Burgundian partisan, Franquet d'Arras, a brigand held in execration throughout the whole north of France. The king's bailli claimed him, in order to hang him. At first she refused, thinking to exchange him; but, at last, consented to give him up to justice. He had deserved hanging a hundred times over. Nevertheless, the having given up a prisoner, the having consented to the death of a human being, must have lowered, even in the eyes of her own party, her character for sanctity.

Unhappy condition of such a soul, fallen upon the realities of this world! Each day she must have lost something of herself. One does not suddenly become rich, noble, honored, the equal of lords and princes, with impunity. Rich dress, letters of nobility, royal favor — all this could not fail at the last to have altered her heroic simplicity. She had obtained for her native village exemption from taxes, and the king had bestowed on one of her brothers the provostship of Vaucouleurs.

But the greatest peril for the saint was from her own sanctity,—from the respect and adoration of the people. At Lagny, she was besought to restore a child to life. The count d'Armagnac wrote, begging her to decide which of the two popes was to be followed. According to the reply she is said to have given (falsified, perhaps), she promised to deliver her decision at the close of the war, confiding in her internal voices to enable her to pass judgment on the very head of authority.

And yet there was no pride in her. She never gave herself out for a saint: often, she confessed that she knew not the future. The evening before a bat-tle she was asked whether the king would conquer, and replied that she knew not. At Bourges, when the women prayed her to touch crosses and chaplets, she began laughing, and said to dame Marguerite, at whose house she was staying, "Touch them yourself, they will be just as good."

The singular originality of this girl was, as we have said, good sense in the midst of exaltation; and this, as we shall see, was what rendered her judges implacable. The pedants, the reasoners who hated her as an inspired being, were so much the more cruel to her from the impossibility of despising her as a mad woman, and from the frequency with which her loftier reason silenced their arguments.

It was not difficult to foresee her fate. She mistrusted it herself. From

the outset she had said—"Employ me,
I shall last but the year, or little
longer." Often, addressing her chaplain, brother Pasquerel, she repeated,
"If I must die soon, tell the king, our
lord, from me, to found chapels for the
offering up of prayers for the salvation of such as have died in defence of
the kingdom."

Her parents asking her, when they
saw her again at Rheims, whether she
had no fear of any thing, her answer
was, "Nothing, except treason."

Often, on the approach of evening,
if there happened to be any church
near the place where the army en-
camped, and particularly, if it belonged to the Mendicant orders, she
gladly repaired to it, and would join
the children who were being prepared
to receive the sacrament. According
to an ancient chronicle, the very day

on which she was fated to be made prisoner, she communicated in the church of St. Jacques, Compiègne, where, leaning, sadly against a pillar, she said to the good people and children who crowded the church — "My good friends and my dear children, I tell you of a surety, there is a man who has sold me; I am betrayed, and shall soon be given up to death. Pray to God for me, I beseech you; for I shall no longer be able to serve my king or the noble realm of France."

The probability is, that the Pucelle was bargained for and bought, even as Soissons had just been bought. At so critical a moment, and when their young king was landing on French ground, the English would be ready to give any sum for her. But the Burgundians longed to have her in their grasp, and they succeeded: it was to the interest not of the duke only and of the Burgundian party in general, but it was, besides, the direct interest of John of Ligny, who eagerly bought the prisoner.

For the Pucelle to fall into the hands of a noble lord of the house of Luxembourg, of a vassal of the chivalrous Duke of Burgundy, of the *good* duke, as he was called, was a hard trial for the chivalry of the day. A prisoner of war, a girl, so young a girl, and, above all, a maid, what had she to fear amidst loyal knights? Chivalry was in every one's mouth as the protection of afflicted dames and damsels. Marshal Boucicaut had just founded an order which had no other object. Besides, the worship of the Virgin, constantly extending in the middle age, having become the dominant religion, it seemed as if virginity must be an inviolable safeguard.

To explain what is to follow, we must point out the singular want of harmony which then existed between ideas and morals, and, however shocking the contrast, bring face to face with the too sublime ideal, with the Imitation, with the Pucelle, the low realities of the time; we must (beseeching pardon of the chaste girl who forms the subject of this narrative) fathom the depths of this world of covetousness and of concupiscence. Without seeing it as it existed, it would be impossible to understand how knights could give up her who seemed the living embodiment of chivalry, how, while the Virgin reigned, the Virgin should show herself, and be so cruelly mistaken.

The religion of this epoch was less

the adoration of the Virgin than of woman; its chivalry was that portrayed in the Petit Jehan de Saintré — but with the advantage of chastity, in favor of the romance, over the truth.

Princes set the example. Charles VII. receives Agnes Sorel as a present from his wife's mother the old queen of Sicily; and mother, wife, and mistress, he takes them all with him, as he marches along the Loire, the happiest understanding subsisting between the three.

The English, more serious, seek love in marriage only. Gloucester marries Jacqueline; among Jacqueline's ladies his regards fall on one, equally lovely and witty, and he marries her too.

But, in this respect, as in all others, France and England are far outstripped by Flanders, by the Count of Flanders, by the great Duke of Burgundy. The legend expressive of the Low Countries, is that of the famous countess who brought into the world three hundred and sixty-five children. The princes of the land, without going quite so far, seem, at the least, to endeavor to approach her. A count of Clèves has sixty-three bastards. John of Burgundy, bishop of Cambrai, officiates pontifically, with his thirty-six bastards and sons of bastards ministering with him at the altar.

Philippe-le-Bon had only sixteen bastards, but he had no fewer than twenty-seven wives, three lawful ones and twenty-four mistresses. In these sad years of 1429 and 1430, and during the enactment of this tragedy of the Pucelle's, he was wholly absorbed in the joyous affair of his third marriage. This time, his wife was an

Infanta of Portugal, English by her mother's side, her mother having been Philippa of Lancaster; so that the English missed their point in giving him the command of Paris, as detain him they could not; he was in a hurry to quit this land of famine, and to return to Flanders to welcome his young bride. Ordinances, ceremonies, festivals, concluded, or interrupted and resumed, consumed whole months. At Bruges, in particular, unheard-of galas took place, rejoicings fabulous to tell of, insensate prodigalities which ruined the nobility — and the burgesses eclipsed them. The seventeen nations which had their warehouses at Bruges, displayed the riches of the universe. The streets were hung with the rich and soft carpets of Flanders. For eight days and eight nights the choicest wines ran in torrents; a stone lion poured forth Rhenish, a stag, Beaune wine; and at meal-times, a unicorn spouted out rose-water and malvoise.

But the splendor of the Flemish feast lay in the Flemish women, in the triumphant beauties of Bruges, such as Rubens has painted them in his Magdalen, in his Descent from the Cross. The Portuguese could not have delighted in seeing her new subjects: already had the Spaniard, Joan of Navarre, been filled with spite at the sight, exclaiming, against her will, " I see only queens here."

On his wedding day (January 10th, 1430), Philippe-le-Bon instituted the order of the Golden Floece, "won by Jason," taking for device the conjugal and reassuring words, *"Autre n'au-ray."* (No other will I have.)

Did the young bride believe in this?

It is dubious. This Jason's, or Gideon's fleece (as the Church soon baptized it,) was, after all, the golden fleece, reminding one of the gilded waves, of the streaming yellow tresses which VanDyck, Philippe-le-Bon's great painter, flings amorously round the shoulders of his saints. All saw in the new order the triumph of the fair, young, flourishing beauty of the north, over the sombre beauties of the south. It seemed as the Flemish prince, to console the Flemish dames, addressed this device of double meaning, " *Autre n'auray,*" to them.

Under these forms of chivalry, awkwardly imitated from romances, the history of Flanders at this period is nevertheless one fiery, joyous, brutal, bacchanalian revel. Under color of tournays, feats of arms, and feasts of the Round Table, there is one wild whirl of light and common gallantries, low intrigues, and interminable junketings. The true device of the epoch is that presumptuously taken by the sire de Ternant at the lists of Arras: —" *Que j'aie de mes désirs assouvissance, et jamais d'autre bien.*" (Let my desires be satisfied, I wish no other good.)

The suprising part of all this is, that amidst these mad festivals and this ruinous magnificence, the affairs of the Count of Flanders seemed to go on all the better. The more he gave, lost, and squandered, the more flowed into him. He fattened and was enriched by the general ruin. In Holland alone he met with any obstacle; but without much trouble he acquired the positions commanding the Somme and the Meuse — Namur and Peronne. Besides the latter town, the English placed in his hands Bar-sur-Seine, Auxerre, Meaux, the approaches to Paris, and lastly, Paris itself.

Advantage after advantage, Fortune piled her favors upon him, without leaving him time to draw breath between her gifts. She threw into the power of one of his vassals the Pucelle, that precious gage for which the English would have given any sum. And, at this very moment, his situation became complicated by another of Fortune's favors, for the duchy of Brabant devolved to him; but he could not take possession of it without securing the friendship of the English.

The death of the Duke of Brabant, who had talked of marrying again, and of raising up heirs to himself, happened just in the nick of time for the Duke of Burgundy. He had acquired almost all the provinces which bound Brabant — Flanders, Hainault, Holland, Namur, and Luxembourg, and only lacked the central province, that is, rich Louvain, with the key to the whole, Brussels. Here was a strong temptation: so, passing over the rights of his aunt, from whom, however, he derived his own, he also sacrificed the rights of his wards, and his own honor and probity as a guardian, and seized Brabant. Therefore, to finish matters with Holland and Luxembourg, and to repulse the Liégeois who had just laid siege to Namur, he was necessitated to remain on good terms with the English; in other words, to deliver up the Pucelle.

Philippe-le-*Bon* (good) was a good man, according to the vulgar idea of goodness, tender of heart, especially to women, a good son, a good father, and with tears at will. He wept over the slain at Azincourt; but his league with the English cost more lives than Azincourt. He shed torrents of tears at his father's death; and then, to avenge him, torrents of blood. Sensibility and sensuality often go together; but sensuality and concupiscence are not the less cruel when aroused. Let the desired object draw back; let concupiscence see her fly and conceal herself from its pursuit, then it turns to blind rage. . . . Woe to whatever opposes it! . . . The school of Rubens, in its Pagan bacchanalia, rejoices in bringing together tigers and satyrs, "lust hard by hate."

He who held the Pucelle in his hands, John of Ligny, the Duke of Burgundy's vassal, found himself precisely in the same situation as his suzerain; like him, it was his hour of cupidity, of extreme temptation. He belonged to the glorious house of Luxembourg, and to be of kin to the emperor Henry VII., and to king John of Bohemia, was an honor well worth preserving unsullied; but John of Ligny was poor, the youngest son of a youngest son. He had contrived to get his aunt, the rich countess of Ligny and of Saint-Pol, to name him her sole heir, and this legacy, which lay exceedingly open to question, was about to be disputed by his eldest brother. In dread of this, John became the docile and trembling servant of the Duke of Burgundy, of the English, and of every one. The English pressed him to deliver up his prisoner to them; and, indeed, they could easily have seized her in the tower of Beaulieu, in Picardy, where they had placed her. But, if he gave her up to them, he would ruin himself with the

Duke of Burgundy, his suzerain, and the judge in the question of his inheritance, who, consequently, could ruin him by a single word. So he sent her, provisorily, to his castle of Beaurevoir, which lay within the territory of the empire.

The English, wild with hate and humiliation, urged and threatened. So great was their rage against the Pucelle, that they burned a woman alive for speaking well of her. If the Pucelle herself were not tried, condemned, and burned as a sorceress — if her victories were not set down as due to the devil, they would remain in the eyes of the people miracles, God's own works. The inference would be, that God was against the English, that they had been rightfully and loyally defeated, and that their cause was the devil's. According to the notions of the time, there was no medium. A conclusion like this, intolerable to English pride, was infinitely more so to a government of bishops, like that of England, and to the cardinal, its head.

Matters were in a desperate state when Winchester took them in hand. Gloucester being reduced to a cipher in England, and Bedford in France, he found himself uncontrolled. He had fancied that on bringing the young king to Calais (April 23d), all would flock to him: not an Englishman budged. He tried to pique their honor by fulminating an ordinance "against those who fear the enchantments of the Pucelle:" it had not the slightest effect. The king remained at Calais, like a stranded vessel. Winchester became eminently ridiculous. After the crusade for the recovery of the Holy Land had dwindled down in his hands to a crusade against Bohemia, he had cut down the latter to a crusade against Paris. This bellicose prelate, who had flattered himself that he should officiate as a conqueror in Notre-Dame, and crown his charge there, found all the roads blocked up. Holding Compiègne, the enemy barred the route through Picardy, and holding Louviers, that through Normandy. Meanwhile the war dragged slowly on, his money wasted away, and the crusade dissolved in smoke. Apparently the Devil had to do with the matter; for the cardinal could only get out of the scrape by bringing the deceiver to his trial; by burning him in the person of the Pucelle.

He felt that he must have her, must force her out of the hands of the Burgundians. She had been made prisoner May 23d; by the 26th a message is dispatched from Rouen, in the name of the vicar of the Inquisition, summoning the Duke of Burgundy and John of Ligny to deliver up this woman, suspected of sorcery. The Inquisition had not much power in France; its vicar was a poor and very timorous monk, a Dominican, and, undoubtedly, like all the other Mendicants, favorable to the Pucelle. But he was here, at Rouen, overawed by the all-powerful cardinal, who held the sword to his breast; and who had just appointed captain of Rouen a man of action, and a man devoted to himself, the earl of Warwick, Henry's tutor. Warwick held two posts, assuredly widely different from one another, but both of great trust; the tutelage of the king, and the care of the king's enemy; the education of the one, the superintendence of the trial of the other.

The monk's letter was a document of little weight, and the University was made to write at the same time. It was hardly possible that the heads of the University should lend any hearty aid to expediting a process instituted by the Papal Inquisition, at the very moment they were going to declare war on the people at Bâle, on behalf of the episcopacy. Winchester himself, the head of the English episcopacy, must have preferred a trial by bishops, or, if he could, to bring bishops and inquisitors to act in concert together. Now he had in his train and among his adherents, a bishop just fitted for the business, a beggared bishop, who lived at his table, and who assuredly would sentence or would swear just as was wanted.

Pierre Cauchon, bishop of Beauvais, was not a man without merit. 'Born at Rheims, near Gerson's place of birth, he was a very influential doctor of the University, and a friend of Clemengis, who asserts that he was both "good and beneficent." This goodness did not hinder him from being one of the most violent of the violent Cabochien party; and as such he was driven from Paris in 1413. He reëntered the capital with the Duke of Burgundy, became bishop of Beauvais, and, under the English rule, was elected by the University conservator of its privileges. But the invasion of northern France by Charles VII., in 1429, was fatal to Cauchon, who sought to keep Beauvais in the English interests, and was thrust out by the citizens. He did not enjoy himself at Paris with the dull Bedford, who had no means of rewarding zeal; and repaired to the fount of wealth and power in England, to Cardinal Winchester. He became English, he spoke English. Winchester perceived the use to which such a man might be put, and attached him to himself by doing for him even more than he could have hoped for. The archbishop of Rouen having been translated elsewhere, he recommended him to the pope to fill that great see. But neither the pope nor the chapter would have any thing to do with Cauchon; and Rouen, at war at the time with the University of Paris, could not well receive as its archbishop a member of that University. Here was a complete stop; and Cauchon stood with gaping mouth in sight of the magnificent prey, ever in hopes that all obstacles would disappear before the invincible cardinal, full of devotion to him, and having no other God.

It was exceedingly opportune that the Pucelle should have been taken close to the limits of Cauchon's diocese; not, it is true, within the diocese itself; but there was a hope of making it believed to be so. So Cauchon wrote, as judge ordinary, to the king of England, to claim the right of trying her; and, on the 12th of June, the University received the king's letters to the effect that the bishop and the inquisitor were to proceed to try her with concurrent powers. Though the proceedings of the Inquisition were not the same as those of the ordinary tribunals of the Church, no objection was raised. The two jurisdictions choosing thus to connive at each other, one difficulty alone remained; the accused was still in the hands of the Burgundians.

The University put herself forward, and wrote anew to the Duke of Burgundy and John of Ligny. Couchon, in his zeal, undertook to be the agent of the English, their courier, to carry the letter himself, and deliver it to the two dukes; at the same time, as bishop, he handed them a summons, calling upon them to deliver up to him a prisoner over whom he claimed jurisdiction. In the course of this strange document of his, he quits the character of judge for that of negotiator, and makes offers of money, stating that although this woman cannot be considered a prisoner of war, the king of England is ready to settle a pension of two or three hundred livres on the bastard of Vendome, and to give the sum of six thousand livres to those who have her in their keeping: then, towards the close of this missive of his, he raises his offer to ten thousand, but pointing out emphatically the magnitude of the offer, "As much," he says, "as the French are accustomed to give for a king or a prince."

The English did not rely so implicitly on the steps taken by the University, and on Cauchon's negotiations, as to neglect the more energetic means. On the same day that the latter presented his summons, or the day after, the council in England placed an embargo on all traffic with the markets of the Low Countries, and, above all, with Antwerp (July 19), prohibiting the English merchants from purchasing linens there, and the other goods for which they were in the habit of exchanging their wool. This was inflicting on the Duke of Burgundy,

Count of Flanders, a blow in the most
sensible part, through the medium of
the great Flemish manufactures, linens and cloth: the English discontinued purchasing the one, and supplying
the material for the other.

While the English were thus stren-
uously urging on the destruction of
the Pucelle, did Charles VII. take any
steps to save her? None, it appears:
yet he had prisoners in his hands, and
could have protected her by threatening reprisals. A short time before, he
had set negotiations on foot through
the medium of his chancellor, the archbishop of Rheims; but neither he nor
the other politicians of the council had
ever regarded the Pucelle with much
favor. The Anjou-Lorraine party, with
the old queen of Sicily, who had taken
her by the hand from the first, could
not, at this precise juncture, interfere

on her behalf with the Duke of Burgundy. The Duke of Lorraine was on his death-bed, the succession to the duchy disputed before the breath was out of his body, and Philippe-le-Bon was giving his support to a rival of Réné of Anjou's, — son-in-law and heir to the Duke of Lorraine.

Thus, on every side, interest and covetousness declared against the Pucelle, or produced indifference to her. The good Charles VII. did nothing for her, the good Duke Philippe delivered her up. The house of Anjou coveted Lorraine, the Duke of Burgundy coveted Brabant; and, most of all, he desiderated the keeping open the trade between Flanders and England. The little had their interests to attend to as well. John of Ligny looked to inherit Saint-Pol, and Cauchon was grasping at the archbishopric of Rouen.

In vain did John of Ligny's wife throw herself at his feet, in vain did she supplicate him not to dishonor himself. He was no longer a free man, already had he touched English gold; though he gave her up, not, it is true, directly to the English, but to the Duke of Burgundy. This house of Ligny and of Saint-Pol, with its recollections of greatness and its unbridled aspirations, was fated to pursue fortune to the end—to the Grève. The surrenderer of the Pucelle seems to have felt all his misery; he had painted on his arms a camel succumbing under its burden, with the sad device, unknown to men of heart, " Nul n'est tenu à l'impossible," (No one is held to impossibilities).

What was the prisoner doing the while? Her body was at Beaurevoir, her soul at Compiègne; she was fighting, soul and spirit, for the king who had deserted her. Without her, she felt that the faithful city of Compiègne would fall, and, with it, the royal cause throughout the North. She had previously tried to effect her escape from the towers of Beaulieu; and at Beaurevoir she was still more strongly tempted to fly: she knew that the English demanded that she should be given up to them, and dreaded falling into their hands. She consulted her saints, and could obtain no other answer than that it behooved to be patient, "that her delivery would not be until she had seen the king of the English." "But," she said within herself, "can it be that God will suffer these poor people of Compiègne to die, who have been, and who are, so loyal to their lord?" Presented under this form of lively compassion, the temptation prevailed. For the first time she turned a deaf ear to her saints: she threw herself from the tower, and fell at its foot half-dead. Borne in again and nursed by the ladies of Ligny, she longed for death, and persisted in remaining two days without eating.

Delivered up to the Duke of Burgundy, she was taken to Arras, and then to the donjon-keep of Crotoy, which has long been covered by the sands of the Somme. From this place of confinement she looked out upon the sea, and could sometimes descry the English downs — that hostile land into which she had hoped to carry war for the deliverance of the Duke of Orléans. Mass was daily performed here by a priest who was also a prisoner, and Jeanne prayed ardently; she asked, and it was given unto her.

9

Though confined in prison, she displayed her power all the same; as long as she lived, her prayers broke through the walls, and scattered the enemy.

On the very day that she had predicted, forewarned by the archangel, the siege of Compiègne was raised — that is, on the 1st of November. The Duke of Burgundy had advanced as far as Noyon, as if to meet and experience the insulting reverse personally. He sustained another defeat shortly afterwards at Germigny (November 20). Saintrailles then offered him battle at Peronne, which he declined.

These humiliations undoubtedly confirmed the duke in his alliance with the English, and determined him to deliver up the Pucelle to them. But the mere threat of interrupting all commercial relations would have been enough.

Chivalrous as he believed himself to be, and the restorer of chivalry, the Count of Flanders was at bottom the servant of the manufacturers and the merchants. The manufacturing cities and the flax-spinning districts would not have allowed commerce to be long interrupted, or their works brought to a stand-still, but would have burst forth into insurrection.

At the very moment the English had got possession of the Pucelle, and were free to proceed to her trial, their affairs were going on very badly. Far from retaking Louviers, they had lost Chateau-galliard. La Hire took it by escalade, and finding Barbazan a prisoner there, set that formidable captain at liberty. The towns voluntarily went over to Charles VII., the inhabitants expelling the English: those of

Melun, close as the town is to Paris, thrust the garrison out of the gates.

To put on the drag, if it were possible, while the affairs of England were thus going rapidly down-hill, some great and powerful engine was necessary, and Winchester had one at hand —the trial and the coronation. These two things were to be brought into play together, or rather, they were one and the same thing. To dishonor Charles VII., to prove that he had been led to be crowned by a witch, was bestowing so much additional sanctity on the coronation of Henry VI.; if the one were avowedly the anointed of the Devil, the other must be recognized as the anointed of God.

Henry made his entry into Paris on the 2d of December. On the 21st of the preceding month, the University had been made to write to Cauchon, complaining of his delays, and beseeching the king to order the trial to be begun. Cauchon was in no haste; perhaps, thinking it hard to begin the work before the wage was assured, and it was not till a month afterwards that he procured from the chapter of Rouen authority to proceed in that diocese. On the instant (January 3, 1431), Winchester issued an ordinance, in which the king was made to say, " that on the requisition of the bishop of Beauvais, and exhorted thereto by his dear daughter, the University of Paris, he commanded her keepers to *conduct* the accused to the bishop." The word was chosen to show that the prisoner was not given up to the ecclesiastical judge, but only lent, " to be taken back again if not convicted." The English ran no risk, she could not escape death; if fire failed, the sword remained.

Cauchon opened the proceedings at Rouen, on the 9th of January, 1431. He seated the vicar of the Inquisition near himself, and began by holding a sort of consultation with eight doctors, licentiates or masters of arts of Rouen, and by laying before them the inquiries which he had instituted touching the Pucelle, but which, having been conducted by her enemies, appeared insufficient to these legists of Rouen. In fact, they were so utterly insufficient, that the prosecution, which, on these worthless data, was about to have been commenced against her on the charge of *magic*, was instituted on the charge of *heresy*.

With the view of conciliating these recalcitrating Normans, and lessening their superstitious reverence for the

forms of procedure, Cauchon nomi-
nated one of their number, Jean de la
Fontaine, examining counsellor (*con-
seiller examinateur*). But he reserved
the most active part, that of promoter
of the prosecution (*promoteur du
procès*), for a certain Estivet, one of
his Beauvais canons by whom he was
accompanied. He managed to con-
sume a month in these preparations;
but the young king having been at
length taken back to London (February 9), Winchester, tranquil on this
head, applied himself earnestly to the
business of the trial, and would trust
no one to superintend it. He thought,
and justly, that the master's eye is the
best, and took up his residence at
Rouen in order to watch Cauchon at
work.

His first step was to make sure of
the monk who represented the Inqui-

sition. Cauchon, having assembled his assessors, Norman priests and doctors of Paris, in the house of a canon, sent for the Dominican, and called upon him to act as his coadjutor in the proceedings. The shaveling timidly replied, that "if his powers were judged sufficient, he would act as his duty required." The bishop did not fail to declare that his powers were amply sufficient; on which the monk further objected, "that he was anxious not to act as yet, both from scruples of conscience and for legality of the trial," and begged the bishop to substitute some one in his place, until he should ascertain that his powers were really sufficient.

His objections were useless; he was not allowed so to escape, and had to sit in judgment, whether he would or not. There was another motive, besides fear, which undoubtedly assisted in keeping him to his post — Winchester assigned him twenty gold sous for his pains. Perhaps, the Mendicant monk had never seen such a quantity of gold in his life.

TRIAL OF THE PUCELLE.

On February 21, the Pucelle was brought before her judges. The bishop of Beauvais admonished her " with mildness and charity," praying her to answer truly to whatever she should be asked, without evasion or subterfuge, both to shorten her trial and ease her conscience. *Answer.* " I do not know what you mean to question me about, you might ask me things which I would not tell you." She consented to swear to speak the truth upon all matters, except those which related to her visions; " But, with respect to these," she said, "you shall cut off my head first." Nevertheless, she was induced to swear that she would answer all questions "on points affecting faith."

She was again urged on the following day, the 22d, and again on the 24th, but held firm. "It is a common remark even in children's mouths," was her observation, "that *people are often hung for telling the truth.*" At last, worn out, and for quietness' sake, she consented to swear "to tell what she knew *upon her trial*, but not all she knew."

Interrogated as to her age, name, and surname, she said that she was about nineteen years old. "In the place where I was born,* they called

---

* Domremy in Champagne, on the frontiers of Burgundy would be distinguished in Joan's time from France Proper.—Translator.

me Jehanette, and in France Jehanne.
. . .'' But, with regard to her surname (the *Pucelle*, the maid), it seems,
that through some caprice of feminine
modesty she could not bring herself to
utter it, and that she eluded the direct
answer by a chaste falsehood — " As
to surname, I know nothing of it."

She complained of the fetters on
her limbs; and the bishop told her that
as she had made several attempts to
escape, they had been obliged to put
them on. " It is true," she said, " I
have done so, and it is allowable for
any prisoner. If I escaped, I could
not be raproached with having broken
my word, for I had given no promise."

She was ordered to repeat the *Pater*
and the *Ave*, perhaps in the superstitious idea that if she were vowed to
the devil she durst not — " I will willingly repeat them if my lord of Beau-

vais will hear me confess:" adroit and touching demand; by thus reposing her confidence in her judge, her enemy, she would have made him both her spiritual father and the witness of her innocence.

Cauchon declined the request; but I can well believe that he was moved by it. He broke up the sitting for that day, and on the day following did not continue the interrogatory himself, but deputed the office to one of his assessors.

At the fourth sitting she displayed unwonted animation. She did not conceal her having heard her voices: "They awakened me," she said, "I clasped my hands in prayer, and besought them to give me counsel; they said to me, 'Ask of our Lord.'" — "And what more did they say?" — " To answer you boldly."

" . . . I cannot tell all; I am much more fearful of saying any thing which may displease them, than I am of answering you. . . . For to-day, I beg you to question me no further."

The bishop, perceiving her emotion, persisted: " But, Jehanne, God is offended, then, if one tells true things?" — " My voices have told me certain things, not for you, but for the king." Then she added, with fervor, " Ah! if he knew them, he would eat his dinner with greater relish. . . . Would that he did know them, and would drink no wine from this to Easter."

She gave utterance to some sublime things, while prattling in this simple strain: " I come from God, I have naught to do here; dismiss me to God, from whom I come. . . ."

" You say that you are my judge; think well what you are about, for of a truth I am sent of God, and you are putting yourself in great danger."

There can be no doubt such language irritated the judges, and they put to her an insidious and base question, a question which it is a crime to put to any man alive: "Jehanne, do you believe yourself to be in a state of grace?"

They thought they had bound her with an indissoluble knot. To say no, was to confess herself unworthy of having been God's chosen instrument; but, on the other hand, how say yes? Which of us, frail beings as we are, is sure here below of being truly in God's grace? Not one, except the proud, presumptuous man, who, of all, is precisely the furthest from it.

She cut the knot, with heroic and Christian simplicity: —

"If I am not, may God be pleased

to receive me into it: if I am, may God be pleased to keep me in it."

The Pharisees were struck speechless.

But, with all her heroism, she was nevertheless a woman. . . . After giving utterance to this sublime sentiment, she sank from the high-wrought mood, and relapsed into the softness of her sex, doubting of her state, as is natural to a Christian soul, interrogating herself, and trying to gain confidence: "Ah! if I knew that I were not in God's grace, I should be the most wretched being in the world. . . . But, if I were in a state of sin, no doubt the voice would not come. . . . Would that every one could hear it like myself. . . ."

These words gave a hold to her judges. After a long pause, they returned to the charge with redoubled hate, and pressed upon her question after question designed to ruin her. "Had not the voices told her to *hate* the Burgundians?" . . . "Did she not go when a child to the *Fairies'* tree?" etc. . . . They now longed to burn her as a witch.

At the fifth sitting she was attacked on delicate and dangerous ground, namely, with regard to the appearances she had seen. The bishop, become all of a sudden compassionate and honied, addressed her with— "Jehanne, how have you been since Saturday?"—"You see," said the poor prisoner, loaded with chains; "as well as I might."

"Jehanne, do you fast every day this Lent?"—"Is the question a necessary one?"—"Yes, truly." "Well then, yes, I have always fasted."

She was then pressed on the subject of her visions, and with regard to a sign shown the dauphin, and concerning St. Catherine and St. Michael. Among other insidious and indelicate questions, she was asked whether, when St. Michael appeared to her, he *was naked?* . . . To this shameful question she replied, without understanding its drift, and with heavenly purity, "Do you think, then, that our Lord has not wherewith to clothe him?"

On March 3, other out-of-the-way questions were put to her, in order to entrap her into confessing some diabolical agency, some evil correspondence with the devil. "Has this Saint Michael of yours, have these holy women, a body and limbs? Are you sure the figures you see are those of angels?" — "Yes, I believe so, as firmly as I believe in God." This answer was carefully noted down.

They then turn to the subject of her wearing male attire, and of her standard. "Did not the soldiery make standards in imitation of yours? Did they not replace them with others?" — "Yes, when the lance (staff) happened to break." — "Did you not say that those standards would bring them luck?" — "No; I only said, 'Fall boldly upon the English,' and I fell upon them myself."

"But why was this standard borne at the coronation, in the church of Rheims, rather than those of the other captains? . . ." "It had seen all the danger, and it was only fair that it should share the honor."

"What was the impression of the people who kissed your feet, hands, and garments?" — "The poor came

to me of their own free-will, because
I never did them any harm, and assisted and protected them, as far as
was in my power."

It was impossible for heart of man
not to be touched with such answers.
Cauchon thought it prudent to proceed henceforward with only a few
assessors on whom he could rely, and
quite quietly. We find the number
of assessors varying at each sitting
from the very beginning of the trial:
some leave, and their places are taken
by others. The place of trial is similarly changed. The accused, who at
first is interrogated in the hall of the
castle of Rouen, is now questioned in
prison. " In order not to fatigue the
rest," Cauchon took there only two
assessors and two witnesses, (from the
10th to the 17th of March.) He was,
perhaps, emboldened thus to proceed

with shut doors, from being sure of the support of the Inquisition; the vicar having at length received from the Inquisitor-General of France full powers to preside at the trial along with the bishop (March 12).

In these fresh examinations, she is pressed only on a few points indicated beforehand by Cauchon.

"Did the voices command her to make that sally out of Compiègne in which she was taken?" To this she does not give a direct reply: "The saints had told me that I should be taken before midsummer; that it behooved so to be, that I must not be astonished, but suffer all cheerfully, and God would aid me. . . . Since it has so pleased God, it is for the best that I should have been taken."

"Do you think you did well in setting out without the leave of your father and mother? Ought we not to honor our parents?"—"They have forgiven me."—"And did you think you were not sinning in doing so?"—"It was by God's command; and if I had had a hundred fathers and mothers I should have set out."

"Did not the voices call you daughter of God, daughter of the Church, the maid of the great heart?" —"Before the siege of Orléans was raised, and since then, the voices have called me, and they call me every day, 'Jehanne the Pucelle, daughter of God.'"

"Was it right to attack Paris, the day of the Nativity of Our Lady?"—"It is fitting to keep the festivals of Our Lady; and it would be so, I truly think, to keep them every day."

"Why did you leap from the tower of Beaurevoir?" (the drift of this question was to induce her to say that she had wished to kill herself.) — "I heard that the poor people of Compiègne would all be slain, down to children seven years of age, and I knew, too, that I was sold to the English; I would rather have died than fall into the hands of the English."

"Do St. Catherine and St. Margaret hate the English?" — "They love what our Lord loves, and hate what he hates." — "Does God hate the English?" — "Of the love or hate God may bear the English, and what he does with their souls, I know nothing; but I know that they will be put forth out of France, with the exception of such as shall perish in it."

"Is it not a mortal sin to hold a man to ransom, and then put him to death?" — "I have not done that." — "Was not Franquet d'Arras put to death ? " — " I consented to it, having been unable to exchange him for one of my men; he owned to being a brigand and a traitor. His trial lasted a fortnight, before the bailli of Senlis." — " Did you not give money to the man who took him ? " — " I am not treasurer of France, to give money."

" Do you think that your king did well in killing, or causing to be killed, my lord of Burgundy ? " — " It was a great pity for the realm of France; but, whatever might have been between them, God sent me to the aid of the king of France."

" Jehanne, has it been revealed to you whether you will escape ? " — " That does not bear upon your trial. Do you want me to depone against myself ? " — " Have the voices said nothing to you about it ? " — " That does not concern your trial; I put myself in our Lord's hands, who will do as it pleaseth him." . . . And, after a pause, "By my troth, I know neither the hour nor the day. God's will be done." — "Have not your voices told you any thing about the result, generally?" — "Well then, yes; they have told me that I shall be delivered, and have bade me be of good cheer and courage. . . ."

Another day she added: "The saints tell me that I shall be victoriously delivered, and they say to me besides, 'Take all in good part; care not for thy martyrdom; thou shalt at the last enter the kingdom of Paradise.'" — "And since they have told you so, do you feel sure of being saved, and of not going to hell?" — "Yes, I believe what they have told me as firmly as if I were already saved." — "This assurance is a very weighty one." — "Yes, it is a great treasure to me." — " And so, you believe you can no longer commit a mortal sin ? " — "I know nothing of that; I rely altogether on our Lord."

At last, the judges had made out the true ground on which to bring the accusation; at last, they had found a spot on which to lay stronghold. There was not a chance of getting this chaste and holy girl to be taken for a witch, for a familiar of the devil's; but, in her very sanctity, as is invariably the case with all mystics, there was a side left open to attack: the secret voice considered equal, or preferred to, the instruction of the Church, the prescriptions of authority — inspiration, but free and independent inspiration — revelation, but a personal revelation — submission to God; what God ? the God within.

These preliminary examinations were concluded by a formal demand, whether she would submit her actions and opinions to the judgment of the Church; to which she replied, "I love the Church, and would support it to the best of my power. As to the good works which I have wrought, I must refer them to the King of heaven, who sent me."

The question being repeated, she gave no other answer, but added, "Our Lord and the Church, it is all one."

She was then told, that there was a distinction; that there was the Church *triumphant*, God, the saints, and those who had been admitted to salvation; and the Church *militant*, or, in other words, the pope, the cardinals, the clergy, and all good Christians — the which Church, "properly assembled,"

cannot err, and is guided by the Holy
Ghost. "Will you not then submit
yourself to the Church *militant?*" —
"I am come to the king of France
from God, from the Virgin Mary, the
saints, and the Church *victorious* there
above; to that Church I submit myself, my works, all that I have done or
have to do." — "And to the Church
militant?" — "I will give no other
answer."

According to one of the assessors
she said that, on certain points, she
trusted to neither bishop, pope, nor
any one; but held her belief of God
alone.

The question on which the trial was
to turn was thus laid down in all its
simplicity and grandeur, and the true
debate commenced: on the one hand,
the visible Church and authority, on
the other, inspiration attesting the

invisible Church; . . . invisible to vulgar eyes, but clearly seen by the pious girl, who was forever contemplating it, forever hearing it within herself, forever carrying in her heart these saints and angels. . . . There was her Church, there God shone in his brightness; everywhere else, how shadowy He was! . . .

Such being the case at issue, the accused was doomed to irremediable destruction. She could not give way; she could not, save falsely, disavow, deny what she saw and heard so distinctly. On the other hand, could authority remain authority if it abdicated its jurisdiction; if it did not punish? The Church militant is an armed Church, armed with a two-edged sword; against whom? Apparently, against the refractory.

Terrible was this Church in the

person of the reasoners, the scholastics, the enemies of inspiration; terrible and implacable, if represented by the bishop of Beauvais. But were there, then, no judges superior to this bishop? How could the episcopal party, the party of the University, fail, in this peculiar case, to recognize as supreme judge its Council of Bâle, which was on the eve of being opened? On the other hand, the papal Inquisition, and the Dominican who was its vicar, would undoubtedly be far from disputing the superiority of the pope's jurisdiction to its own, which emanated from it.

A legist of Rouen, that very Jean de la Fontaine who was Cauchon's friend and the enemy of the Pucelle, could not feel his conscience at ease in leaving an accused girl, without counsel, ignorant that there were judges of appeal, on whom she could call without any sacrifice of the ground on which she took up her defence. Two monks likewise thought that a reservation should be made in favor of the supreme right of the pope. However irregular it might be for assessors to visit and counsel the accused, apart from their coadjutors, these three worthy men, who saw Cauchon violate every legal form for the triumph of iniquity, did not hesitate to violate all forms themselves for justice's sake, intrepidly repaired to the prison, forced their way in, and advised her to appeal. The next day, she appealed to the pope and to the council. Cauchon, in his rage, sent for the guards and inquired who had visited the Pucelle. The legist and the two monks were in great danger of death. From that day they disappear from among the assessors, and with them the last semblance of justice disappears from the trial.

Cauchon, at first, had hoped to have on his side the authority of the lawyers, which carried great weight at Rouen. But he had soon found out that he must do without them. When he showed the minutes of the opening proceedings of the trial to one of these grave legists, master Jehan Lohier, the latter plainly told him that the trial amounted to nothing; that it was all informal; that the assessors were not free to judge; that the proceedings were carried on with closed doors; that the accused, a simple country girl, was not capable of answering on such grave subjects and to learned doctors; and, finally, the lawyer had the boldness to say to the churchman, " The proceedings are, in point of fact, instituted to impugn the honor of the prince, whose side this girl espouses; you shall cite him to appear as well, and assign him an advocate." This intrepid gravity, which recalls Papinian's bearing towards Caracalla, would have cost Lohier dear; but the Norman Papinian did not, like the other, calmly wait the death-stroke on his curule chair; he set off at once for Rome, where the pope eagerly attached such a man to himself, and appointed him one of the judges of the Holy See: he died, dean of the Rota.

Apparently, Cauchon ought to have been better supported by the theologians. After the first examinations, armed with the answers, which she had given against herself, he shut himself up with his intimates, and availing himself, especially, of the pen of an able member of the University of Paris, he drew from these answers a few counts, on which the opinion of the leading doctors and of the ecclesiastical bodies was to be taken. This was the detestable custom, but in reality (whatever has been said to the contrary) the common and regular way of proceeding in inquisitorial trials. These propositions, extracted from the answers given by the Pucelle, and drawn up in general terms, bore a false show of impartiality; although, in point of fact, they were a caricature of those answers, and the doctors consulted could not fail to pass an opinion upon them, in accordance with the hostile intention of their iniquitous framers.

But, however the counts might be framed — however great the terror which hung over the doctors consulted, they were far from being unanimous in their judgments. Among these doctors, the true theologians, the sincere believers, those who had preserved the firm faith of the middle age, could not easily reject this tale of celestial appearances, of visions; for then they might have doubted all the marvels of the lives of the saints, and discussed all their legends. The venerable bishop of Avranches replied, on being consulted, that, according to the teaching of St. Thomas, there was nothing impossible in what this girl affirmed, nothing to be lightly rejected.

The bishop of Lisieux, while acknowledging that Jeanne's revelations might be the work of the devil, humanely added, that they might also be *simple lies*, and that if she did not submit herself to the Church, she must be adjudged schismatic, and be vehemently *suspected* in regard to faith.

Many legists answered like true Normans, by finding her guilty and most guilty, *except she acted by God's command.* One bachelor at law went further than this; while condemning her, he demanded, in consideration of the weakness of her sex, *that the twelve propositions should be read over to her* (he suspected, and with reason, that they had not been communicated to her), and that they should then be laid before the pope — this would have been adjourning the matter indefinitely.

The assessors, assembled in the chapel of the archbishopric, had decided against her on the showing of these propositions. The chapter of Rouen, likewise consulted, was in no haste to come to a decision, and to give the victory to the man it detested and trembled at having for its archbishop; but chose to wait for the reply from the University of Paris, which had been applied to on the subject. There could be no doubt what this reply would be; the Gallican party, that is, the University and scholàstic party, could not be favorable to the Pucelle; an individual of this party, the bishop of Coutances, went beyond all others in the harshness and singularity of his answer. He wrote to the bishop of Beauvais, that he considered the accused to be wholly the devil's, "because she was without the two qualities required by St. Gregory,— virtue and humanity," and that her assertions were so heretical, that though she should revoke them, she must nevertheless be held in strict keeping.

It was a strange spectacle to see
these theologians, these doctors, laboring with all their might to ruin the
very faith which was the foundation
of their doctrine, and which constituted the religious principle of the
middle age in general,—belief in revelations; in the intervention of supernatural beings. . . . They might have
their doubts as to the intervention of
angels; but their belief in the devil's
agencies was implicit.

And was not the important question
whether internal revelations ought to
be hushed, and to disavow themselves
at the Church's bidding, was not this
question, so loudly debated in the
outer world, silently discussed in the
inner world, in the soul of her who
affirmed and who believed in their
existence the most firmly of all?
Was not this battle of faith fought

in the very sanctuary of faith? fought in this loyal and simple heart? . . . I have reason to believe so.

At one time she expressed her readiness to submit herself to the pope, and asked to be sent to him. At another she drew a distinction, maintaining that as regarded *faith* she acknowledged the authority of the pope, the bishops, and the Church, but, as regarded what she had *done*, she could own no other judge than God. Sometimes, making no distinction, and offering no explanation, she appealed " to her King, to the judge of heaven and of earth."

Whatever care has been taken to throw these things into the shade, and to conceal this, the human side, in a being who has been fondly painted as all divine, her fluctuations are visible; and it is wrong to charge her judges with having misled her so as to make her prevaricate on those questions. "She was very subtle," says one of the witnesses, and truly; "of a woman's subtlety." I incline to attribute to these internal struggles the sickness which attacked her, and which brought her to the point of death; nor did she recover, as she herself informs us, until the period that the angel Michael, the angel of battles, ceased to support her, and gave place to Gabriel, the angel of grace and of divine love.

She fell sick in Passion week. Her temptation began, no doubt, on Palm Sunday.* A country girl, born on the

---

* "I know not why," says a great spiritual teacher, "God chooses the most solemn festivals to try and to purify his elect. . . . It is above only, in the festival of heaven, that we shall be delivered from all our troubles." — Saint-Cyran, in the Mèmoires de Lancelot, i. 61.

skirts of a forest, and having ever lived in the open air of heaven, she was compelled to pass this fine Palm Sunday in the depths of a dungeon. The grand *succor* which the Church invokes * came not for her; the *doors did not open.*†

They were opened on the Tuesday; but it was to lead the accused to the great hall of the castle before her judges. They read to her the articles which had been founded on her answers, and the bishop previously represented to her, "that these doctors

---

* The office for prime, on this day runs: "Deus, in *adjutorium* meum intende. . . ." (Come, O God, to my aid.)

† Every one knows that the service for this festival is one of those in which the beautiful dramatic forms of the middle age have been preserved. The procession finds the door of the church shut, the minister knocks: "Attollite portas. . . ." And *the door is opened* to the Lord.

were all churchmen, clerks, and well-read in law, divine and human; that they were all tender and pitiful, and desired to proceed mildly, seeking neither vengance *nor corporal punishment,* but solely wishing to enlighten her, and put her in the way of truth and of salvation; and that, as she was not sufficiently informed in such high matters, the bishop and the inquisitor offered her the choice of one or more of the assessors to act as her counsel." The accused, in presence of this assembly, in which she did not descry a single friendly face, mildly answered, " For what you admonish me as to my good, and concerning our faith, I thank you; as to the counsel you offer me, I have no intention to forsake the counsel of our Lord."

The first article touched the capital point, submission. She replied as before, "Well do I believe that our Holy Father, the bishops, and others of the Church, are to guard the Christian *faith*, and punish those who are found wanting. As to my *deeds* (faits), I submit myself only to the Church in heaven, to God and the Virgin, to the sainted men and women in Paradise. I have not been wanting in regard to the Christian faith, and trust I never shall be."

And, shortly afterwards: "I would rather die than recall what I have done by our Lord's command."

What illustrates the time, the uninformed mind of these doctors, and their blind attachment to the letter without regard to the spirit, is, that no point seemed graver to them than the sin of having assumed male attire. They represented to her that, according to the canons, those who thus change the habit of their sex are abominable in the sight of God. At first she would not give a direct answer, and begged for a respite till the next day; but her judges insisting on her discarding the dress, she replied, "That she was not empowered to say when she could quit it."—"But if you should be deprived of the privilege of hearing mass?"—"Well, our Lord can grant me to hear it without you."—"Will you put on a woman's dress, in order to receive your Saviour at Easter?"—"No; I cannot quit this dress; it matters not to me in what dress I receive my Saviour."— After this she seems shaken, asks to be at least allowed to hear mass, adding, "I won't say but if you were to give me a gown such as the daughters of the burghers wear, a very *long gown. . . .*"

It is clear she shrank, through modesty, from explaining herself. The poor girl durst not explain her position in prison, or the constant danger she was in. The truth is, that three soldiers slept in her room,* three of the brigand ruffians called *houspilleurs;* that she was chained to a beam by a large iron chain,† almost wholly at their mercy; the man's dress they wished to compel her to discontinue was all her safeguard. . . . What are

* Five Englishmen; three of whom stayed at night in her room. (*Houspiller,* is to worry like a dog — hence the name *Houspilleur*). Notices des MSS. iii. 506.

† "She slept with double chains round her limbs, and closely fastened to a chain traversing the foot of her bed, attached to a large piece of wood five or six feet long, and padlocked, so that she could not stir from the place." — Ibidem. Another witness states: "There was an iron beam, to keep her straight (*erectam*)." *Proces MS.,* Evidence of Pierre Cusquel.

we to think of the imbecility of the judge, or of his horrible connivance?

Besides being kept under the eyes of these wretches, and exposed to their insults and mockery, * she was subjected to espial from without. Winchester, the inquisitor, and Cauchon † had each a key to the tower,

---

* The Count de Ligny went to see her with an English lord, and said to her, "Jeanne, I come to hold you to ransom, provided you promise never again to bear arms against us." She replied: "Ah! my God, you are laughing at me; I know you have neither the will nor the power." And when he repeated the words, she added, "I am convinced these English will put me to death, in the hope of winning the kingdom of France. But though the *Godons* (Goddens) should be a hundred thousand more than they are to-day, they would not win the kingdom." The English lord was so enraged that he drew his dagger to plunge it into her, but was hindered by the earl of Warwick. Notices des MSS. iii. 371.

† Not precisely Cauchon, but his man, Estivet, promoter of the prosecution. Ibid. iii. 473.

and watched her hourly through a hole in the wall. Each stone of this infernal dungeon had eyes.

Her only consolation was, that she was at first allowed interviews with a priest, who told her that he was a prisoner, and attached to Charles VIIth's cause. Loyseleur, so he was named, was a tool of the English. He had won Jeanne's confidence, who used to confess herself to him; and, at such times, her confessions were taken down by notaries concealed on purpose to overhear her. . . . It is said that Loyseleur encouraged her to hold out, in order to insure her destruction. On the question of her being put to the torture being discussed (a very useless proceeding, since she neither denied nor concealed any thing), there were only two or three of her judges who counselled the atrocious deed, and the confessor was one of these.

The deplorable state of the prisoner's health was aggravated by her being deprived of the consolations of religion during Passion Week. On the Thursday, the sacrament was withheld from her: on that self-same day on which Christ is universal host, on which He invites the poor and all those who suffer, she seemed to be *forgotten.**

On Good Friday, that day of deep silence, on which we all hear no other sound than the beating of one's own heart, it seems as if the hearts of the judges smote them, and that some feeling of humanity and of religion had been awakened in their aged

* "Usque quo *oblivisceres* me in finem?" (How long wilt thou forget me?) Service for Holy Thursday, Lauds.

scholastic souls: at least it is certain, that whereas thirty-five of them took their seats on the Wednesday, no more than nine were present at the examination on Saturday: the rest, no doubt, alleged the devotions of the day as their excuse.

On the contrary, her courage had revived. Likening her own sufferings to those of Christ, the thought had roused her from her despondency. She answered, when the question was again put to her, "that she would defer to the Church militant, *provided it commanded nothing impossible.*" — "Do you think, then, that you are not subject to the Church which is upon earth, to our holy father the pope, to the cardinals, archbishops, bishops, and prelates?" — "Yes, certainly, *our Lord served.*" — "Do your voices forbid your submitting to the Church militant?"—"They do not forbid it, *our Lord being served first.*"

This firmness did not desert her once on the Saturday: but on the next day, the Sunday, Easter Sunday! what must her feelings have been? What must have passed in that poor heart, when the sounds of the universal holiday enlivening the city, Rouen's five hundred bells ringing out with their joyous peals on the air,* and the whole Christian world coming to life with the Saviour, she remained with death!

Summon up our pride as much as we may, philosophers and reasoners as we boast ourselves to be in this present age, but which of us — amidst the agitations of modern bustle and excitement, or, in the voluntary cap-

* Compare the statement, given above, as to the deep impression made on her by the sound of bells.

tivity of study, plunged in its toilsome and solitary researches, which of us hears without emotion the sounds of these beautiful Christian festivals, the touching voice of the bells, and, as it were, their mild maternal reproach? . . . Who can see, without envying them, those crowds of believers issuing from the Church, made young again and revived by the divine table? . . . The mind remains firm, but the soul is sad and heavy. . . . He who believes in the future, and whose heart is not the less linked to the past, at such moments lays down the pen, closes the book, and cannot refrain from exclaiming "Ah! why am I not with them, one of them, and the simplest, the least of these little children!"

What must have been one's feelings at that time, when the Christian world

was still one, still undivided! What
must have been the throes of that
young soul which had lived but on
faith? . . . Could she who, with all
her inner life of visions and revelations, had not the less docilely obeyed
the commands of the Church; could
she, who till now had believed herself
in her simplicity "a good girl," as she
said, a girl altogether submissive to
the Church — could she without terror
see the Church against her? Alone,
when all are united with God — alone
excepted from the world's gladness
and universal communion, on the day
on which the gates of heaven are
opened to mankind — alone to be ex-
cluded! . . .

And was this exclusion unjust?
. . . The Christian's soul is too humble ever to pretend that it has a right
to receive its God. . . . After all,

what, who was she, to undertake to gainsay these prelates, these doctors? How dared she speak before so many able men — men who had studied? Was there not presumption and damnable pride in an ignorant girl's opposing herself to the learned? a poor, simple girl, to men in authority? . . . Undoubtedly fears of the kind agitated her mind.

On the other hand, this opposition is not Jeanne's, but that of the saints and angels who have dictated her answers to her, and, up to this time, sustained her. . . . Wherefore, alas! do they come no more in this pressing need of hers? Wherefore do those consoling countenances of the saints appear no more, except in a doubtful light, and growing paler daily? . . . Wherefore is the so long-promised deliverance delayed? . . . Doubtless the prisoner has put these questions to herself over and over again; doubtless, silently, gently, she has over and over again quarrelled with her saints and angels. But angels who do not keep their word, can they be angels of light? . . . Let us hope that this horrible thought did not occur to her mind.

There was one means of escaping: this was, without expressly disavowing, to forbear affirming, and to say, "It seems to me." The lawyers thought it easy for her to pronounce these few simple words; but in her mind, to use so doubtful an expression was in reality equivalent to a denial; it was abjuring her beautiful dream of heavenly friendships, betraying her sweet sisters on high. . . . Better to die. . . . And, indeed, the unfortunate, rejected by the visible, abandoned by the invisible Church, by the world, and by her own heart, was sinking. . . . And the body was following the sinking soul. . . .

It so happened that on that very day she had eaten part of a fish which the charitable bishop of Beauvais had sent her, and might have imagined herself poisoned. The bishop had an interest in her death; it would have put an end to this embarrassing trial, would have got the judge out of the scrape: but this was not what the English reckoned upon. The earl of Warwick, in his alarm, said, "The *king* would not have her by any means die a natural death. The *king* has bought her dear. . . . She must die by justice and be burnt. . . . See and cure her."

All attention, indeed, was paid her; she was visited and bled, but was none the better for it, remaining weak and nearly dying. Whether through fear that she should escape thus and die without retracting, or that her bodily weakness inspired hopes that her mind would be more easily dealt with, the judges made an attempt while she was lying in this state (April 18). They visited her in her chamber, and represented to her that she would be in great danger if she did not reconsider, and follow the advice of the Church. "It seems to me, indeed," she said, "seeing my sickness, that I am in great danger of death. If so, God's will be done; I should like to confess, receive my Saviour, and be laid in holy ground." — "If you desire the sacraments of the Church, you must do as good Catholics do, and submit yourself to it." She made no reply. But, on the judge's repeating his words,

she said: " If the body die in prison,
I hope that you will lay it in holy
ground; if you do not, I appeal to
our Lord."

Already, in the course of these examinations, she had expressed one of
her last wishes. *Question.* " You
say that you wear a man's dress by
God's command, and yet, in case you
die, you want a woman's shift?" —
Answer. " All I want is to have a
long one." This touching answer
was ample proof that, in this extremity, she was much less occupied
with care about life than with the
fears of modesty.

The doctors preached to their
patient for a long time; and he who
had taken on himself the especial care
of exhorting her, master Nicolas Midy,
a scholastic of Paris, closed the scene
by saying bitterly to her: " If you

don't obey the Church, you will be abandoned for a Saracen."—"I am a good Christian," she replied meekly, "I was properly baptized, and will die like a good Christian."

The slowness of these proceedings drove the English wild with impatience. Winchester had hoped to have been able to bring the trial to an end before the campaign; to have forced a confession from the prisoner, and have dishonored king Charles. This blow struck, he would recover Louviers, secure Normandy and the Seine, and then repair to Bâle to begin another war,—a theological war,—to sit there as arbiter of Christendom, and make and unmake popes. At the very moment he had these high designs in view, he was compelled to cool his heels, waiting upon what it might please this girl to say.

The unlucky Cauchon happened at this precise juncture to have offended the chapter of Rouen, from which he was soliciting a decision against the Pucelle: he had allowed himself to be addressed beforehand, as "My lord, the archbishop." Winchester determined to disregard the delays of these Normans, and to refer at once to the great theological tribunal, the University of Paris.

While waiting for the answer, new attempts were made to overcome the resistance of the accused; and both stratagem and terror were brought into play. In the course of a second admonition (May 2), the preacher, master Châtillon, proposed to her to submit the question of the truth of her visions to persons of her own party. She did not give in to the snare. "As to this," she said, "I depend on my Judge, the King of heaven and earth." She did not say this time, as before, " On God and *the pope.*" — " Well, the Church will give you up, and you will be in danger of fire, both soul and body. You will not do what we tell you, until you suffer body and soul."

They did not stop at vague threats. On the third admonition, which took place in her chamber (May 11), the executioner was sent for, and she was told that the torture was ready. . . . But the manœuvre failed. On the contrary, it was found that she had resumed all, and more than all her courage. Raised up after temptation, she seemed to have mounted a step nearer the source of grace. " The angel Gabriel," she said, " has appeared to strengthen me; it was he, my saints have assured me so. . . .

God has been ever my master in what I have done; the devil has never had power over me. . . . Though you should tear off my limbs and pluck my soul from my body, I would say nothing else." The spirit was so visibly manifested in her that her last adversary, the preacher Châtillon was touched, and became her defender, declaring that a trial so conducted seemed to him null. Cauchon, beside himself with rage, compelled him to silence.

The reply of the University arrived at last. The decision to which it came on the twelve articles was, that this girl was wholly the devil's; was impious in regard to her parents; thirsted for Christian blood, &c. This was the opinion given by the faculty of theology. That of law was more moderate, declaring her to be deserv-

ing of punishment, but with two res-
ervations — 1st, in case she persisted
in her non-submission; 2d, if she
were in her right senses.

At the same time, the University
wrote to the pope, to the cardinals,
and to the king of England, lauding
the bishop of Beauvais, and setting
forth, " that there seemed to it to have
been great gravity observed, and a
holy and just way of proceeding,
which ought to be most satisfactory
to all."

Armed with this response, some of
the assessors were for burning her
without further delay; which would
have been sufficient satisfaction for
the doctors, whose authority she rejected, but not for the English who
required a retraction that should
defame *(infamât)* king Charles. They
had recourse to a new admonition and

a new preacher, master Pierre Morice, which was attended by no better result. It was in vain that he dwelt upon the authority of the University of Paris, "which is the light of all science." — "Though I should see the executioner and the fire there," she exclaimed, " though I were in the fire, I could only say what I have said."

It was by this time the 23d of May, the day after Pentecost; Winchester could remain no longer at Rouen, and it behooved to make an end of the business. Therefore, it was resolved to get up a great and terrible public scene, which should either terrify the recusant into submission, or, at the least, blind the people. Loyseleur, Châtillon, and Morice, were sent to visit her the evening before, to promise her that if she would submit and quit her man's dress, she should be delivered out of the hands of the English, and placed in those of the Church.

This fearful farce was enacted in the cemetery of Saint-Ouen, behind the beautifully severe monastic church so called; and which had by that day assumed its present appearance. On a scaffolding raised for the purpose sat cardinal Winchester, the two judges, and thirty-three assessors, of whom many had their scribes seated at their feet. On another scaffold, in the midst of *huissiers* and tortures, was Jeanne, in male attire, and also notaries to take down her confessions, and a preacher to admonish her; and, at its foot, among the crowd, was remarked a strange auditor, the executioner upon his cart, ready to bear her off as soon as she should be adjudged his.

The preacher on this day, a famous doctor, Guillaume Erard, conceived himself bound, on so fine an opportunity, to give the reins to his eloquence; and by his zeal he spoiled all. "O, noble house of France," he exclaimed, "which wast ever wont to be protectress of the faith, how hast thou been abused to ally thyself with a heretic and schismatic. . . ." So far the accused had listened patiently, but when the preacher, turning towards her, said to her, raising his finger, "It is to thee, Jehanne, that I address myself, and I tell thee that thy king is a heretic and schismatic," the admirable girl, forgetting all her danger, burst forth with, "On my faith, sir, with all due respect, I undertake to tell you, and to swear, on pain of my life, that he is the noblest Christian of all Christians, the sincerest lover of the faith and of the Church, and not what you call him." — "Silence her," called out Cauchon.

Thus all these efforts, pains, and expense, had been thrown away. The accused adhered to what she had said. All they could obtain from her, was her consent to submit herself *to the pope.* Cauchon replied, " The pope is too far off." He then began to read the sentence of condemnation, which had been drawn up beforehand, and in which, among other things, it was specified : " And furthermore, you have obstinately persisted in refusing to submit yourself *to the Holy Father* and to the Council," &c. Meanwhile, Loyseleur and Erard conjured her to have pity on herself; on which the bishop, catching at a shadow of hope, discontinued his reading. This drove the English mad; and one of Winchester's secretaries told Cauchon it was clear that he favored the girl — a charge repeated by the cardinal's chaplain. "Thou art a liar," exclaimed the bishop. "And thou," was the retort, "art a traitor to the king." These grave personages seemed to be on the point of going to cuffs on the judgment-seat.

Erard, not discouraged, threatened, prayed. One while he said, "Jehanne, we pity you so. . . . !" and another, "Abjure, or be burnt!" All present evinced an interest in the matter, down even to a worthy catchpole (*huissier*), who, touched with compassion, besought her to give way, assuring her that she should be taken out of the hands of the English and placed in those of the Church. "Well, then," she said, "I will sign." On this, Cauchon, turning to the cardinal, respectfully inquired what was to be done next. "Admit her to do penance," replied the ecclesiastical prince.

Winchester's secretary drew out of his sleeve a brief revocation, only six lines long, (that which was given to the world took up six pages,) and put a pen in her hand, but she could not sign. She smiled, and drew a circle: the secretary took her hand, and guided it to make a cross.

The sentence of grace was a most severe one: — "Jehanne, we condemn you, out of our grace and moderation, to pass the rest of your days in prison, on the bread of grief and water of anguish, and so to mourn your sins."

She was admitted by the ecclesiastical judge to do penance, no doubt, nowhere save in the prisons of the church. The ecclesiastic *in pace,* however severe it might be, would at the least withdraw her from the hands of the English, place her under shelter from their insults, save her honor. Judge of her surprise and despair when the bishop coldly said: "Take her back whence you brought her."

Nothing was done; deceived on this wise, she could not fail to retract her retractation. Yet, though she had abided by it, the English, in their fury, would not have allowed her so to escape. They had come to Saint-Ouen in the hope of at last burning the sorceress, had waited panting and breathless to this end; and now they were to be dismissed on this fashion, paid with a slip of parchment, a signature, a grimace. . . . At the very moment the bishop discontinued reading the sentence of condemnation, stones flew upon the scaffolding without any respect for the cardinal. . . . The doctors were in peril of their lives as they came down from their séats into the public place; swords were in all directions pointed at their throats. The more moderate among the English confined themselves to insulting language: "Priests, you are not earning the king's money." The doctors, making off in all haste, said tremblingly: "Do not be uneasy, we shall soon have her again."

And it was not the soldiery alone, not the English *mob*, always so ferocious, which displayed this thirst for blood. The better born, the great, the lords, were no less sanguinary. The king's man, his tutor, the earl of Warwick, said like the soldiers: "The king's business goes on badly: the girl will not be burnt."

According to English notions, Warwick was the mirror of worthiness, the accomplished Englishman, the perfect *gentleman.* Brave and devout, like his master, Henry V., and the zealous champion of the *established* Church, he had performed the pilgrimage to the Holy Land, as well as many other chivalrous expeditions, not failing to give tournays on his route: one of the most brilliant and celebrated of which took place at the gates of Calais, where he defied the whole chivalry of France. This tournay was long remembered; and the bravery and magnificence of this Warwick served not a little to prepare the way for the famous Warwick, the *king-maker.*

With all his chivalry, Warwick was

not the less savagely eager for the
death of a woman, and one who was,
too, a prisoner of war. The best, and
the most looked-up-to of the English,
was as little deterred by honorable
scruples as the rest of his countrymen from putting to death on the
award of priests, and by fire, her who
had humbled them by the sword.

This great English people, with so
many good and solid qualities, is in-
fected by one vice, which corrupts
these very qualities themselves. This
rooted, all-poisoning vice, is pride: a
cruel disease, but which is nevertheless the principle of English life, the
explanation of its contradictions, the
secret of its acts. With them, virtue
or crime is almost ever the result of
pride; even their follies have no other
source. This pride is sensitive, and
easily pained in the extreme; they are

great sufferers from it, and again, make it a point of pride to conceal these sufferings. Nevertheless, they will have vent. The two expressive words, *disappointment* and *mortification*, are peculiar to the English language.

This self-adoration, this internal worship of the creature for its own sake, is the sin by which Satan fell; the height of impiety. This is the reason that with so many of the virtues of humanity, with their seriousness and sobriety of demeanor, and with their biblical turn of mind, no nation is further off from grace. They are the only people who have been unable to claim the authorship of the Imitation of Jesus: a Frenchman might write it, a German, an Italian, never an Englishman. From Shakspeare to Milton, from Milton to

Byron, their beautiful and sombre lite-
rature is skeptical, Judaical, satanic,
in a word, antichristian. " As regards
law," as a legist well says, " the English are Jews, the French Christians."
A theologian might express himself in
the same manner, as regards faith.
The American Indians, with that pene-
tration and originality they so often
exhibit, expressed this distinction in
their fashion. " Christ," said one of
them, " was a Frenchman whom the
English crucified in London; Pontius
Pilate was an officer in the service of
Great Britain."

The Jews never exhibited the rage
against Jesus which the English did
against the Pucelle. It must be
owned that she had wounded them
cruelly in the most sensible part —
in the simple but deep esteem they
have for themselves. At Orléans, the

invincible men-at-arms, the famous archers, Talbot at their head, had shown their backs; at Jargeau, sheltered by the good walls of a fortified town, they had suffered themselves to be taken; at Patay, they had fled as fast as their legs would carry them, fled before a girl. . . . This was hard to be borne, and these taciturn English were forever pondering over the disgrace. . . . They had been afraid of a girl, and it was not very certain but that, chained as she was, they felt fear of her still. . . . though, seemingly, not of her, but of the Devil, whose agent she was. At least, they endeavored both to believe, and to have it believed so.

But there was an obstacle in the way of this, for she was said to be a virgin; and it was a notorious and well-ascertained fact, that the devil could not make a compact with a virgin. The coolest head among the English, Bedford, the regent, resolved to have the point cleared up; and his wife, the duchess, intrusted the matter to some matrons, who declared Jehanne to be a maid : * a favorable declaration which turned against her, by giving rise to another superstitious notion; to wit, that her virginity constituted her strength, her power, and that to deprive her of it was to disarm her, was to break the charm, and lower her to the level of other women.

The poor girl's only defence against such a danger had been wearing male attire; though, strange to say, no one

* Must it be said that the Duke of Bedford, so generally esteemed as an honorable and well-regulated man, "saw what took place on this occasion, concealed," (erat in quodam loco secreto ubi videbat Joannam visitari). Notices des MSS. iii. 372.

had ever seemed able to understand her motive for wearing it. All, both friends and enemies, were scandalized by it. At the outset, she had been obliged to explain her reasons to the woman of Poitiers; and when made prisoner, and under the care of the ladies of Luxembourg, those excellent persons prayed her to clothe herself as honest girls were wont to do. Above all, the English ladies, who have always made a parade of chastity and modesty, must have considered her so disguising herself monstrous, and insufferably indecent. The duchess of Bedford sent her female attire; but by whom? by a man, a tailor. The fellow, with impudent familiarity, was about to pass it over her head, and, when she pushed him away, laid his unmannerly hand upon her; his tailor's hand on that hand

which had borne the flag of France —
she boxed his ear.

If women could not understand this
feminine question, how much less
could priests! . . . They quoted the
text of a council held in the fourth
century, which anathematized such
changes of dress; not seeing that the
prohibition specially applied to a period when manners had been barely
retrieved from pagan impurities. The
doctors belonging to the party of
Charles VII., the apologists of the
Pucelle, find exceeding difficulty in
justifying her on this head. One of
them (thought to be Gerson) makes
the gratuitous supposition that the
moment she dismounted from her
horse, she was in the habit of resuming woman's apparel; confessing that
Esther and Judith had had recourse
to more natural and feminine means

for their triumphs over the enemies of God's people. Entirely pre-occupied with the soul, these theologians seem to have held the body cheap; provided the letter, the written law, be followed, the soul will be saved; the flesh may take its chance. . . . A poor and simple girl may be pardoned her inability to distinguish so clearly.

It is our hard condition here below, that soul and body are so closely bound one with the other, that the soul takes the flesh along with it, undergoes the same hazards, and is answerable for it. . . . This has ever been a heavy fatality; but how much more so does it become under a religious law, which ordains the endurance of insult, and which does not allow imperilled honor to escape by flinging away the body, and taking refuge in the world of spirits!

On the Friday and the Saturday, the unfortunate prisoner, despoiled of her man's dress, had much to fear. Brutality, furious hatred, vengeance, might severally incite the cowards to degrade her before she perished, to sully what they were about to burn. . . . Besides, they might be tempted to varnish their infamy by a *reason of state*, according to the notions of the day — by depriving her of her virginity, they would undoubtedly destroy that secret power of which the English entertained such great dread, who, perhaps, might recover their courage when they knew that, after all, she was but a woman. According to her confessor, to whom she divulged the fact, an Englishman, not a common soldier, but a *gentleman*, a lord — patriotically devoted himself to this execution, bravely undertook to violate a girl laden with fetters, and, being unable to effect his wishes, rained blows upon her.

"On the Sunday morning, Trinity Sunday, when it was time for her to rise (as she told him who speaks), she said to her English guards, 'Leave me, that I may get up.' One of them took off her woman's dress, emptied the bag in which was the man's apparel, and said to her, 'Get up.' — 'Gentlemen,' she said, 'you know that dress is forbidden me; excuse me, I will not put it on.' The point was contested till noon;. when, being compelled to go out for some bodily want, she put it on. When she came back, they would give her no other despite her entreaties." *

* Is it not surprising to find Lingard and Turner suppressing these essential circumstances, and concealing the true cause of the Pucelle's resuming

In reality, it was not to the interest of the English that she should resume her man's dress, and so make null and void a retractation obtained with such difficulty. But at this moment, their rage no longer knew any bounds. Saintrailles had just made a bold attempt upon Rouen. It would have been a lucky hit to have swept off the judges from the judgment-seat, and have carried Winchester and Bedford to Poitiers; the latter was, subsequently, all but taken on his return, between Rouen and Paris. As long as this accursed girl lived, who, beyond a doubt, continued in prison to practice her sorceries, there was no safety for the English: perish, she must.

The assessors, who had notice in-

male attire? In this, both the Catholic and the Protestant historian sink into the mere Englishman.

14

stantly given them of her change of dress, found some hundred English in the court to obstruct their passage ; who, thinking that if these doctors entered, they might spoil all, threatened them with their axes and swords, and chased them out, calling them *traitors of Armagnacs.* Cauchon, introduced with much difficulty, assumed an air of gayety to pay his court to Warwick, and said with a laugh, " She is caught."

On the Monday, he returned along with the inquisitor and eight assessors, to question the Pucelle, and ask her why she had resumed that dress. She made no excuse, but bravely facing the danger, said that the dress was fitter for her as long as she was guarded by men, and that faith had not been kept with her. Her saints, too, had told her, " that it was great

pity she had abjured to save her life."
Still, she did not refuse to resume
woman's dress. "Put me in a seemly
and safe prison," she said, "I will be
good, and do whatever the Church
shall wish."

On leaving her, the bishop encountered Warwick and a crowd of English; and to show himself a good Englishman, he said in their tongue,
"Farewell, farewell." This joyous
adieu was about synonymous with
"Good evening, good evening; all's
over."

On the Tuesday, the judges got up
at the archbishop's palace a court of
assessors as they best might; some of
them had assisted at the first sittings
only, others at none: in fact, com-
posed of men of all sorts, priests,
legists, and even three physicians.
The judges recapitulated to them

what had taken place, and asked their opinion. This opinion, quite different from what was expected, was that the prisoner should be summoned, and her act of abjuration be read over to her. Whether this was in the power of the judges is doubtful. In the midst of the fury and swords of a raging soldiery, there was in reality no judge, and no possibility of judgment. Blood was the one thing wanted; and that of the judges was, perhaps, not far from flowing. They hastily drew up a summons, to be served the next morning at eight o'clock: she was not to appear, save to be burnt.

Cauchon sent her a confessor in the morning, brother Martin l'Advenu, "to prepare her for her death, and persuade her to repentance. . . . And when he apprized her of the death she was to die that day, she began to cry out grievously, to give way, and tear her hair: — 'Alas! am I to be treated so horribly and cruelly? must my body, pure as from birth, and which was never contaminated, be this day consumed and reduced to ashes? Ha! ha! I would rather be beheaded seven times over than be burnt on this wise. . . . Oh! I make my appeal to God, the great judge of the wrongs and grievances done me!'"

After this burst of grief, she recovered herself and confessed! she then asked to communicate. The brother was embarrassed; but consulting the bishop, the latter told him to administer the sacrament, "and whatever else she might ask." Thus, at the very moment he condemned her as a relapsed heretic, and cut her off from the Church, he gave her all that the Church gives to her faithful.

Perhaps a last sentiment of humanity awoke in the heart of the wicked judge: he considered it enough to burn the poor creature, without driving her to despair, and damning her. Perhaps, also, the wicked priest, through freethinking levity, allowed her to receive the sacraments as a thing of no consequence, which, after all, might serve to calm and silence the sufferer. . . . Besides, it was attempted to do it privately, and the eucharist was brought without stole and light. But the monk complained, and the Church of Rouen, duly warned, was delighted to show what it thought of the judgment pronounced by Cauchon; it sent along with the body of Christ numerous torches and a large escort of priests, who sang litanies, and, as they passed through the streets, told the kneeling people, " Pray for her."

After partaking of the communion, which she received with abundance of tears, she perceived the bishop, and addressed him with the words, "Bishop, I die through you. . . ." And, again, "Had you put me in the prisons of the Church, and given me ghostly keepers, this would not have happened. . . . And for this, I summon you to answer before God."

Then, seeing among the bystanders Pierre Morice, one of the preachers by whom she had been addressed, she said to him, "Ah, master Pierre, where shall I be this evening?"—"Have you not good hope in the Lord?"—"Oh! yes; God to aid, I shall be in Paradise."

It was nine o'clock: she was dressed in female attire, and placed on a cart. On one side of her was brother Martin l'Advenu; the constable, Massieu, was on the other. The Augustine monk, brother Isambart, who had already displayed such charity and courage, would not quit her. It is stated that the wretched Loyseleur also ascended the cart, to ask her pardon: but for the earl of Warwick, the English would have killed him.*

Up to this moment the Pucelle had never despaired, with the exception, perhaps, of her temptation in the Passion week. While saying, as she at times would say, "These English will kill me," she in reality did not think so. She did not imagine that she could ever be deserted. She had faith in her king, in the good people of France. She had said expressly, "There will be some disturbance

---

* This, however, is only a *rumor* (Audivit dici. . . .), a dramatic incident, with which popular tradition has, perhaps, gratuitously adorned the tale.

either in prison or at the trial, by which I shall be delivered, . . . greatly, victoriously delivered." . . . But though king and people deserted her, she had another source of aid, and a far more powerful and certain one, from her friends above, her kind and dear saints. . . . When she was assaulting Saint-Pierre, and deserted by her followers, her saints sent an invisible army to her aid. How could they abandon their obedient girl; they who had so often promised her *safety* and *deliverance.* . . .

What then must her thoughts have been, when she saw that she must die; when, carried in a cart, she passed through a trembling crowd, under the guard of eight hundred Englishmen armed with sword and lance. She wept and bemoaned herself, yet reproached neither her king nor her saints. . . . She was only heard to utter, " O Rouen, Rouen ! must I then die here ? "

The term of her sad journey was the old market-place, the fish-market. Three scaffolds had been raised: on one, was the episcopal and royal chair, the throne of the Cardinal of England, surrounded by the stalls of his prelates; on another, were to figure the principal personages of the mournful drama, the preacher, the judges, and the bailli, and, lastly, the condemned one; apart, was a large scaffolding of plaster, groaning under a weight of wood — nothing had been grudged the stake, which struck terror by its height alone. This was not only to add to the solemnity of the execution, but was done with the intent that from the height to which it was reared, the executioner might not get at it save at

the base, and that to light it only, so
that he would be unable to cut short
the torments and relieve the sufferer,
as he did with others, sparing them the
flames. On this occasion, the important point was that justice should not
be defrauded of her due, or a dead
body be committed to the flames; they
desired that she should be really burnt
alive, and that, placed on the summit
of this mountain of wood, and commanding the circle of lances and of
swords, she might be seen from every
part of the market-place. There was
reason to suppose that being slowly,
tediously burnt before the eyes of a
curious crowd, she might at last be
surprised into some weakness, that
something might escape her which
could be set down as a disavowal, at
the least some confused words which
might be interpreted at pleasure, per-

haps, low prayers, humiliating cries for mercy, such as proceed from a woman in despair. . . .

A chronicler, friendly to the English, brings a heavy charge against them at this moment. According to him, they wanted her gown to be burnt first, so that she might remain naked, "in order to remove all the doubts of the people;" that the fagots should then be removed so that all might draw nigh to see her, "and all the secrets which can or should be in a woman:" and that after this immodest, ferocious exhibition, "the executioners should replace the great fire on her poor carrion. . . ."

The frightful ceremony began with a sermon. Master Nicolas Midy, one of the lights of the university of Paris, preached upon the edifying text: "When one limb of the Church is sick, the whole Church is sick." This poor Church could only be cured by cutting off a limb. He wound up with the formula: " Jeanne, *go* in peace, the church can no longer defend *thee*."

The ecclesiastical judge, the bishop of Beauvais, then benignly exhorted her to take care of her soul and to recall all her misdeeds, in order that she might awaken to true repentance. The assessors had ruled that it was the law to read over her abjuration to her; the bishop did nothing of the sort. He feared her denials, her disclaimers. But the poor girl had no thought of so chicaning away life: her mind was fixed on far other subjects. Even before she was exhorted to repentance, she had knelt down and invoked God, the Virgin, St. Michael and St. Catherine, pardoning all and

asking pardon, saying to the bystanders, " Pray for me!" . . . In particular, she besought the priests to say
each a mass for her soul. . . . And all
this, so devoutly, humbly, and touch-
ingly, that sympathy becoming conta-
gious, no one could any longer contain himself; the bishop of Beauvais
melted into tears, the bishop of Bou-
logne sobbed, and the very English
cried and wept as well, Winchester
with the rest.

Might it be in this moment of universal tenderness, of tears, of conta-
gious weakness, that the unhappy girl,
softened, and relapsing into the mere
woman, confessed that she saw clearly
she had erred, and that, apparently,
she had been deceived when promised
deliverance. This is a point on which
we cannot implicitly rely on the inter-
ested testimony of the English. Nev-

ertheless, it would betray scant knowledge of human nature to doubt, with her hopes so frustrated, her having wavered in her faith. . . . Whether she confessed to this effect in words is uncertain; but I will confidently affirm that she owned it in thought.

Meanwhile the judges, for a moment put out of countenance, had recovered their usual bearing, and the bishop of Beauvais, drying his eyes, began to read the act of condemnation. He reminded the guilty one of all her crimes, of her schism, idolatry, invocation of demons, how she had been admitted to repentance, and how, "Seduced by the prince of lies, she had fallen, O grief! *like the dog which returns to his vomit.* . . . Therefore, we pronounce you to be a rotten limb, and, as such, to be lopped off from the Church. We deliver you over to the secular power, praying it at the same time to relax its sentence, and to spare you death, and the mutilation of your members."

Deserted thus by the Church, she put her whole trust in God. She asked for the cross. An Englishman handed her a cross which he made out of a stick; she took it, rudely fashioned as it was, with not less devotion, kissed it, and placed it under her garments, next to her skin. . . . But what she desired was the crucifix belonging to the Church, to have it before her eyes till she breathed her last. The good *hussier*, Massieu, and brother Isambart, interfered with such effect, that it was brought her from St. Sauveur's. While she was embracing this crucifix, and brother Isambart was encouraging her, the English began to think all this exceedingly tedious; it was now noon, at least; the soldiers grumbled, and the captains called out "What's this, priest; do you mean us to dine here?" . . . Then, losing patience, and without waiting for the order from the bailli, who alone had authority to dismiss her to death, they sent two constables to take her out of the hands of the priests. She was seized at the foot of the tribunal by the men-at-arms, who dragged her to the executioner with the words, "Do thy office. . . ." The fury of the soldiery filled all present with horror; and many there, even of the judges, fled the spot that they might see no more.

When she found herself brought down to the market-place, surrounded by English, laying rude hands on her, nature asserted her rights, and the flesh was troubled. Again she cried

15

out, "O Rouen, thou art then to be my last abode! . . ." She said no more, and, in this hour of fear and trouble, *did not sin with her lips.* . . .

She accused neither her king, nor her holy ones. But when she set foot on the top of the pile, on viewing this great city, this motionless and silent crowd, she could not refrain from exclaiming, " Ah! Rouen, Rouen, much do I fear you will suffer from my death!" She who had saved the people, and whom that people deserted, gave voice to no other sentiment when dying (admirable sweetness of soul!) than that of compassion for it.

She was made fast under the infamous placard, mitred with a mitre on which was read — " Heretic, relapser, apostate, idolater. . . ." And then the executioner set fire to the pile. . . . She saw this from above and uttered a cry. . . . Then, as the brother who was exhorting her paid no attention to the fire, forgetting herself in her fear for him, she insisted on his descending.

The proof that up to this period she had made no express recantation is, that the unhappy Cauchon was obliged (no doubt by the high Satanic will which presided over the whole) to proceed to the foot of the pile, obliged to face his victim to endeavor to extract some admission from her. All that he obtained was a few words, enough to rack his soul. She said to him mildly, what she had already said: "Bishop, I die through you. . . . If you had put me into the church prisons, this would not have happened." No doubt hopes had been entertained that on finding herself abandoned by her king, she would at last accuse and defame him. To the last, she defended him: "Whether I have done well or ill, my king is faultless; it was not he who counselled me."

Meanwhile, the flames rose. . . . When they first seized her, the unhappy girl shrieked for holy *water* — this must have been the cry of fear. . . . But soon recovering, she called only on God, on her angels and her saints. She bore witness to them: — "Yes, my voices were from God, my voices have not deceived me." The fact that all her doubts vanished at this trying moment, must be taken as a proof that she accepted death as the promised *deliverance;* that she no longer understood her *salvation* in the Judaic and material sense, as until now she had done, that at length she saw clearly; and that rising above all shadows, her gifts of illumination and of sanctity were at the final hour made perfect unto her.

The great testimony she thus bore is attested by the sworn and compelled witness of her death, by the Dominican who mounted the pile with her, whom she forced to descend, but who spoke to her from its foot, listened to her, and held out to her the crucifix.

There is yet another witness of this sainted death, a most grave witness, who must himself have been a saint. This witness, whose name history ought to preserve, was the Augustine monk already mentioned, brother Isambart de la Pierre. During the trial, he had hazarded his life by counselling the Pucelle, and yet, though so clearly pointed out to the hate of the English, he persisted in accompanying her in the cart, procured the parish crucifix for her, and comforted her in the midst of the raging multitude, both on the scaffold where she was interrogated, and at the stake.

Twenty years afterwards, the two venerable friars, simple monks, vowed to poverty, and having nothing to hope or fear in this world, bear witness to the scene we have just described: "We heard her," they say, "in the midst of the flames invoke her saints, her archangel; several times she called on her Saviour. . . . At the last, as her head sunk on her bosom, she shrieked, 'Jesus!'"

"Ten thousand men wept. . . ." A few of the English alone laughed, or endeavored to laugh. One of the most furious among them had sworn that he would throw a fagot on the pile. Just as he brought it, she breathed her last. He was taken ill.

His comrades led him to a tavern to recruit his spirits by drink, but he was beyond recovery. "I saw," he exclaimed, in his frantic despair, "I saw a dove fly out of her mouth with her last sigh." Others had read in the flames the word "Jesus," which she so often repeated. The executioner repaired in the evening to brother Isambart, full of consternation, and confessed himself; but felt persuaded that God would never pardon him. . . . One of the English king's secretaries said aloud, on returning from the dismal scene, "We are lost; we have burnt a saint."

Though these words fell from an enemy's mouth, they are not the less important, and will live, uncontradicted by the future. Yes, whether considered religiously or patriotically, Jeanne Darc was a saint.

Where find a finer legend than this true history? Still, let us beware of converting it into a legend; let us piously preserve its every trait, even such as are most akin to human nature, and respect its terrible and touching reality. . . .

Let the spirit of romance profane it by its touch, if it dare; poetry will ever abstain. For what could it add? . . . The idea which, throughout the middle age, it had pursued from legend to legend, was found at the last to be a living being — the dream was a reality. The Virgin, succorer in battle, invoked by knights, and looked for from above, was here below. . . . and in whom? Here is the marvel. In what was despised, in what was lowliest of all, in a child, in a simple country girl, one of the poor, of the people of France. . . . For there was a people, there was a France. This last impersonation of the past was also the first of the period that was commencing. In her there at once appeared the Virgin. . . . and, already, country.

Such is the poetry of this grand fact, such its philosophy, its lofty truth. But the historic reality is not the less certain; it was but too positive, and too cruelly verified. . . . This living enigma, this mysterious creature, whom all concluded to be supernatural, this angel or demon, who, according to some, was to fly away some morning, was found to be a woman, a young girl; was found to be without wings, and linked as we ourselves to a mortal body, was to suffer, to die — and how frightful a death !

But it is precisely in this appa-

rently degrading reality, in this sad
trial of nature, that the ideal is dis-
coverable, and shines brightly. Her
contemporaries recognized in the
scene Christ among the Pharisees.
. . . Still we must see in it something
else — the Passion of the Virgin, the
martyrdom of purity.

There have been many martyrs:
history shows us numberless ones,
more or less pure, more or less glorious. Pride has had its martyrs; so
have hate, and the spirit of contro-
versy. No age has been without martyrs militant, who no doubt died with
a good ·grace when they could no
longer kill. . . . Such fanatics are
irrelevant to our subject. The sainted
girl is not of them; she had a sign of
her own — goodness, charity, sweetness of soul.

She had the sweetness of the an-

'cient martyrs, but with a difference. The first Christians remained gentle and pure only by shunning action, by sparing themselves the struggles and the trials of the world. Jehanne was gentle in the roughest struggle, good amongst the bad, pacific in war itself; she bore into war (that triumph of the devil's) the spirit of God.

She took up arms, when she knew "the pity for the kingdom of France." She could not bear to see "French blood flow." This tenderness of heart she showed towards all men. After a victory she would weep, and would attend to the wounded English.

Purity, sweetness, heroic goodness —that this supreme beauty of the soul should have centred in a daughter of France, may suprise foreigners who choose to judge of our nation by the levity of its manners alone. We may tell them (and without partiality, as we speak of circumstances so long since past) that under this levity, and in the midst of its follies and its very vices, old France was not styled without reason, the most Christian people. They were certainly the people of love and of grace; and whether we understand this humanly or Christianly, in either sense it will ever hold good.

The deliverer of France could be no other than a woman. France herself was woman; having her nobility, but her amiable sweetness likewise, her prompt and charming pity; at the least, possessing the virtue of quickly-excited sympathies. And though she might take pleasure in vain elegances and external refinements, she remained at bottom closer to nature. The Frenchman, even when vicious, preserved, beyond the man of every other nation, good sense and goodness of heart. . . .

May new France never forget the saying of old France: "Great hearts alone understand how much glory there is in *being good!*" To be and to keep so, amidst the injuries of man and the severity of Providence, is not the gift of a happy nature alone, but it is strength and heroism. . . . To preserve sweetness and benevolence in the midst of so many bitter disputes, to pass through a life's experiences without suffering them to touch this internal treasure — is divine. They who persevere, and so go on to the end, are the true elect. And though they may even at times have stumbled in the difficult path of the world, amidst their falls, their weaknesses, and their *infancies*, they will not the less remain children of God!

FINIS.